Closing the Gap

English Educators Address the Tensions Between Teacher Preparation and Teaching Writing in Secondary Schools

A volume in
Literacy, Language, and Learning
Patricia Ruggiano Schmidt, *Series Editor*

Literacy, Language, and Learning

Patricia Ruggiano Schmidt, *Le Moyne College*
Series Editor

Closing the Gap: English Teachers Address the Tensions Between Teacher Preparation and Teaching Writing in Secondary Schools (2007)
Edited by Karen Keaton Jackson and Sandra Vavra

African American Middle-Income Parents: How Are They Involved in Their Children's Literacy Development? (2007)
By Ethel Swindell Robinson

Research and Reflection: Teachers Take Action for Literacy Development (2006)
By Andrea Izzo

ABCs of Cultural Understanding and Communication: National and International Adaptations (2005)
Edited by Patricia Ruggiano Schmidt and Claudia Finkbeiner

Preparing Educators to Communicate and Connect with Families and Communities (2005)
Edited by Patricia Ruggiano Schmidt

Reading and Writing Ourselves Into Being: The Literacy of Certain Nineteenth-Century Young Women (2004)
By Claire White Putala

Reconceptualizing Literacy in the New Age of Multiculturalism and Pluralism (2001)
Edited by Patricia Ruggiano Schmidt and Peter B. Mosenthal

Closing the Gap

**English Educators Address
the Tensions Between Teacher Preparation
and Teaching Writing in Secondary Schools**

Edited by

**Karen Keaton Jackson
and
Sandra Vavra**

INFORMATION AGE PUBLISHING, INC.
Charlotte, NC • www.infoagepub.com

Library of Congress Cataloging-in-Publication Data

Closing the gap : English educators address the tensions between teacher preparation and teaching writing in secondary schools / edited by Karen Keaton Jackson and Sandra Vavra.
    p. cm.
 Includes bibliographical references.
 ISBN-13: 978-1-59311-781-8 (pbk.)
 ISBN-13: 978-1-59311-782-5 (hardcover)
 1. English language--Composition and exercises--Study and teaching (Secondary) 2. Effective teaching. I. Jackson, Karen Keaton. II. Vavra, Sandra.
 LB1631.C58 2007
 808'.0420712--dc22

                                            2007027250

Printed in the United States of America

CONTENTS

PART I

Closing Gaps in Teacher Preparation

PART II

Closing Gaps in the Writing Classroom

EDITORS' NOTES

The Competing Rites
and Methodological Rights
of Teaching Writing

While speech is the medium of home and the neighborhood interaction,
writing is largely or completely the medium of the school, and the child whose school
writing is stultified has little else to draw on. . . . A sense of the social system of writing
has so inhibited and overawed many teachers that they have never given a pupil
the feeling that what he writes is his own.

—John Dixon

Despite decades of theorizing, experimenting, and research in writing pedagogy, high school English teachers are more vulnerable than ever to the public's displeasure about the failure to teach students how to use language to communicate effectively. Parents, and taxpayers in general, seem most concerned that students fail to learn about how to spell or use punctuation correctly (mechanics)—which are typically measured on standardized tests and thus lionized as key indicators of writing proficiency. On the other hand, university composition faculty continue to criticize high school teachers for what LaBrant first called the "large gap between natural expression and the stilted performance which passes as school composition" (1934). Even though English educators from five countries proposed a new writing curriculum which featured a process-oriented method at the seminal 1965 Dartmouth Conference, researchers still find that high school teachers continue to focus composition instruction on discrete grammar exercises unrelated to student writing and on the minute correc-

Closing the Gap, pages vii–xv
Copyright © 2007 by Information Age Publishing
All rights of reproduction in any form reserved.

tion of surface errors in writing products as the way to teach writing and prepare students for standardized end-of-course writing tests.

Yet, the National Assessment of Education Progress report card on writing (2002) states that a mere 23% of the nation's fourth graders and only 31% of its eighth graders were rated "proficient" in writing (National Center for Educational Statistics). Additionally, the most recent report from the National Commission on Writing in America's Schools and Colleges (2003) clearly recommends that institutions require teacher education programs to improve writing across all disciplines, since elementary and secondary schools are giving short shrift to writing. It reveals that few states require specific coursework in writing pedagogy to earn licensure and that literacy education is focused on reading instruction, to the detriment of writing. Why? Because there is little correlation between writing and reading competencies. Even though research supports some integration of writing and reading—indeed, even common sense tells us they are opposite sides of the same coin—we can only conclude that the focus on reading has meant that research on writing and writing pedagogy has not been sufficiently shared with pre-service teachers.

Sociocognitive theorists (Bakhtin, 1981; Vygotsky, 1978) have successfully argued the point that we teach what we know, that the twelve years of educational experience preservice teachers bring with them to their teacher-preparation programs have already predisposed them to value certain ways of teaching and learning. Therefore, if their beliefs remain unexamined or unchallenged by new learning, they will continue the cycle of inadequate writing instruction which currently characterizes our schools—a spiralling cycle of inadequacy which could arguably be described as educational malpractice. To put our national writing crisis in terms of the global economy, China will soon become the country with the fifth largest English-speaking population in the world. India already has a sizeable English speaking population. Together, the top twenty percent of IQs among students in their countries accounts for more students than the *total* population of students in the United States. In educational terms, that means they have more *honors* students than we have students altogether. If Chinese and Indian students can communicate in English (particularly in writing) better than our students can, what is to keep high paying jobs—many of which require advanced communication skills—here in the United States?

Yet, can English teachers be blamed? Writing theorists and researchers during the decades since the Dartmouth Conference have argued for the *process model*, the *writing workshop*, and *portfolio assessment* as preferred approaches for teaching writing, all of which assume producing authentic and thoughtful writing requiring protracted work. A short list of seminal compositionists, their key constructs/works, and their interrlationships demonstrates the rich legacy from which current teachers can work as they design curriculum and teach writing:

Foundational Theories about Writing and Key Theorists

(a) James Britton (British Schools Council Project, 1975), borrowed from Vygotsky and Piaget:
Concepts
Three categories about how language functions:

- transactional (language used to get things done)
- expressive (language used to think aloud on paper)
- poetic (language used to create literary patterns)

User, audience, and purpose are interrelated differently in each category; Participants vs. Spectators

Recommendation
Teachers should provide frequent opportunities for expressive writing in English classrooms.

(b) James Moffett (*Teaching the Universe of Discourse*, 1968; *Active Voice*, 1992):
Concepts and Recommendations
Instruction should progress from *conceptualization* to *oral language* to *written language* and from *egocentric communication* to *public discourse*.

Developmental Tasks Theories and Key Theorists

(a) Piaget (not a writing theorist per se, but his observations help teachers understand how the developing mind structures knowledge)
Original Concept
There are four stages of cognitive development: *sensorimotor, preoperational, concrete logical,* and *formal operations.*

Recommendations Derived from Piaget's Stages
Writing instruction should be built on talking and listening, both grounded in thinking.
Writing has developmental stages which parallel cognitive development.
More complex/abstract writing tasks/stages should follow those that are more concrete.
The Developmental Stages of Writing and Their Implications (Moffett's Theory of Communication):

- Teachers should understand the current level of writing competence/comfort of students and then challenge them to move to higher stages.

- The sequence of writing has five stages which should be followed in long-range planning of instruction.
- The stages are *episodic* (nonsequential, not used in elementary school only): *narrative, descriptive, explanatory, analytical, artistic.*
- Each stage requires progressively increasing cognitive complexity and writing competence, preceding stages can be revisited, and growth within stages is ongoing (9–12).
- The National Assessment of Educational Programs (NAEP) supports the Developmental writing sequence by designating three major genres of writing: *narrative, informative,* and *persuasive.*

Process Model Theories and Key Theorists

(a) Atwell, Calkins, Graves, Murray

Assumptions

The writer is a self-starter with a need to communicate ("Everyone has a story to tell"; "no more writer's welfare").

Writing is an extended process.

All modes of writing are equally respected.

Students are expected to write often and to take responsibility for shaping their own writing.

Conferencing is a basic feature of instruction.

Student writers need many readers to respond to their work.

Ownership of writing begins with selecting the topic and extends to giving the writing a public performance.

Writing is a whole process whose parts are recursive.

Comparing product, process, and post-process teaching approaches provides insights helpful to writing teachers.

(b) Murray

Concepts

The teacher's role is *responding* to student writing through mini-lessons, whole-class meetings, and conferences.

The emotional tone of the encounters is encouraging, facilitating, guiding.

The student *acts*, the teacher *reacts*, i.e., only responds to the student's response to his/her own writing (non-directive).

(c) Atwell

Concepts

The teacher's role is a "knowing expert" to the student's role as "apprentice."

The teacher establishes direction for writing assignments and intervenes in writing at key points to tell writers what works and what doesn't work.

(d) Giacobbe (Murray's disciple)

Concepts

The variables of the teacher's role in the process writing model are as follows:

- Everyone is motivated to make meaning.
- All students have potential to write something worthwhile.
- Teachers should teach the process of discovering meaning in experience that students can apply anywhere.
- Teachers should not force deadlines on writing.
- Teaching the craft of writing needs to allow for discovery, trial and error, even some failing.
- There is no specific content to teach before students start writing.
- Teachers serve as coaches to help each writer discover his/her own voice.
- The student teaches the teacher to teach writing through conferences in which the teacher listens to what the student thinks about his/her own writing and then helps the student hear what he/she said.
- The teacher serves as a mirror to help students see their own potential.
- A teacher is a success when students can teach themselves, making the teacher unnecessary.

Writing Workshop

Note: It grew out of the middle-school movement which sought to make these schools less subject driven than high schools and more like the homelike environment of elementary classrooms.

Middle schools are characterized by less content to cover, a slower pace, and non-traditional classroom arrangements. Writing Workshop, like Atwell's and Calkins' classrooms, operate more like newsrooms and artists studios than traditional classrooms with rows of seats and lectures.

Portfolio Work and Key Theorists

(a) Elbow

Concepts

Students should be in charge of their writing.

He invites students to show their best work "so we can see what you know and can do rather than what you don't know and can't do."

Portfolios in writing classrooms cause students to *collect* (gather samples of their literacies, *select* (decide on the best representatives), *reflect* (write about their decisions), and *project* (set writing goals and work to meet them).

Portfolios transfer responsibility, relieving teachers of the burden of reading every piece and giving students some responsibility for the quality and appraisal of their work.

(b) Bromley (1998)

Concepts

Argues for variety in portfolios (e,g., skills checklists, self-assessment pieces, creative writing, letters, reports, and work from a variety of modes).

Authentic Assessment and Key Theorists

General Assumptions

Teachers must establish a clear connection between what is taught and what is being assessed, through clear rubrics which judge student outcomes.

Authentic assessment ensures that writing tasks which are graded are those which actually have been taught.

(a) Resnick; Applebee (New Standards Project)

Concepts

Argues for "direct writing assessment," clearly delineated criteria arrayed along a numbered scale.

Holistic evaluation scores are a grade which expresses a rater's/teacher's assessment of "the extent to which features in a piece of writing appear to be under the control of the writer."

Note 1: There are various rubrics among the states:, e.g., the State of Virginia's multidomain rubric and Pennsylvania's assessment rubric.

Note 2: North Carolina is a leader in authentic assessment (led by former Governor Hunt).

Two features make NC assessment unique:

- standardized writing tests use prompts similar to what people encounter in the workplace/real world.
- levels of performance are defined by rubrics designed to be clear to both students and teachers.

Despite the research-based recommendations made by these proven practitioners—during the same decades they worked—politicians, test-making corporations, and administrators unschooled in relevant writing research have fueled the public demand for teacher accountability and reduced the score card for this accountability largely to high-stakes, end-of-course standardized tests. Since school funding allocations and teacher pay are tied to test scores, is it any wonder that teachers often choose to "teach to the test" rather than teach to the research-based theories that promote real learning about how to write?

As university teachers of composition, teachers of English methods courses, and university supervisors of student teachers, we are acutely aware of the cognitive dissonance our teacher candidates face as they try to implement what they learn at the university about research-based teaching practices like the *process model* in school systems which do not accommodate these practices because of time constraints, curricular demands of teaching additional subject matter like literature, the political and financial bias toward standardized test scores, and the prevailing tradition of teaching composition by means of discrete grammar exercises and multiple-choice testing about language and writing rather than by means of actual writing. Even the best evidence-based recommendations will not be utilized and sustained in practice unless careful thought is given to identifying the conditions that will increase the probability of their successful implementation.

This book invited essays which acknowledge the dilemma of secondary school English teachers and which make practical recommendations about how these teachers can practice research-based writing pedagogy while taking into account the barriers to change in public school policy and practice: the demands of test score accountability, the difficulty of change in school environments, and the often competing demands of stakeholders (parents, testing agencies, university faculty, tax payers in general, school administrators). Contributors to this book have considered the following five interlocking writing constructs, which constitute best teaching practices, as they make recommendations for appropriate classroom practices and activities: (1) the developmental tasks (cognitive tools) required to accomplish successively more difficult tasks; (2) the necessary steps in the writing process; (3) the environment in which different writing tasks can be undertaken and completed (workshop); (4) the roles of teacher and students in determining writing topics and other responsibilities in the classroom (portfolios); and (5) how assignments and evaluation prepare students to meet the needs of everyday writing (authentic assessment). They have also addressed issues that the Dartmouth Conference did not address, but which we have learned through research in the past few decades are essential to teaching excellence, e.g., culturally relevant pedagogy and teacher advocacy on behalf of students (Delpit; Schmidt; Troutman; Villanueva).

It is hoped that the collection of essays in this book serves as a strong voice in support of best practices for teaching writing which accommodate realties and yet advocate for needed changes that will support the overall effectiveness of the instructional delivery system for writing. As professionals, we are tasked to do no less. Not to succeed is to deny our students and the candidates we teach and help license the dignity of finding their own voice and the joy of shaping and expressing their own ideas compellingly.

—Karen Keaton Jackson and Sandra Vavra

WORKS REFERENCED

Applebee, A. N. (1978). *A survey of teaching conditions in English, 1977.* Urbana, IL: NCTE and ERIC/RCS.

Applebee, A. N. (1996). *Curriculum as conversation: Transforming traditions of teaching and learning.* Chicago: University of Chicago Press.

Applebee, A. N. (1997). Rethinking curriculum in the English language arts. *English Journal, 86*(5), 25–31.

Atwell, N. (1987). *In the middle: Writing, reading, and learning with adolescents.* Upper Montclair, NJ: Boynton/Cook.

Atwell, N. (1998). *In the middle: New understandings about writing, reading, and learning* (2nd ed.). Portsmouth, NH: Boynton/Cook & Heinemann.

Bakhtin, M. M. (1981). *The dialogic imagination.* Austin: The University of Texas Press.

Bromley, K. (1998). *Language arts: Exploring connections.* Boston: Allyn & Bacon.

Britton, J., Burgess, T., Martin, N., McLeod, A., & Rosen, H. (1975). *The development of writing abilities: 11–18.* London: Macmillan Education.

Calkins, L. M. (1983). *Lessons from a child: On the teaching and learning of writing.* Exeter, NH: Heinemann.

Calkins, L. M. (1986). *The art of teaching writing.* Portsmouth, NH: Heinemann.

Delpit, L. (1988). The silenced dialogue: Power and pedagogy in educating other people's children. *Harvard Educatinal Review, 58*(3), 280–298.

Delpit, L. (1995). *Other people's children: Cultural conflict in the classroom.* New York: New Press.

Elbow, P. (1973). *Writing without teachers.* New York: Oxford University Press.

Elbow, P. (1986). *Embracing contraries: Explorations in learning and teaching.* New York: Oxford.

Elbow, P., & Belanoff, P. (1986). Portfolios as a substitute for proficiency examination. *College Composition and Communication, 37*(3), 336–339.

Giacobbe, M. E., & Cazden, C. (1986.) *NCTE research report.* Spring Conference, Boston.

Graves, D. H. (1983). *Writing: Teachers and children at work.* Exeter, NH: Heinemann.

Graves, D. H. (1991). *The reading/writing teacher's companion: Build a literate classroom.* Portsmouth, NH: Heinemann.

LaFontana, V. R. (1996.) Throw away that correcting pen. *English Journal, 85*(6), 71–73.

Moffett, J. (1968). *Teaching the universe of discourse.* Boston: Houghton Mifflin.

Moffett, J. (1992.) *Active voice: A writing program across the curriculum* (2nd ed.). Portsmouth, NH: Boynton/Cook.

Murphy, S., & Smith, M. A. (1992.) Looking into portfolios. *Portfolios in the writing classroom.* Urbana, IL: NCTE.

Murray, D. M. (1968). *A writer teaches writing.* Boston: Houghton Mifflin.

Murray, D. M. (1982). *Learning by teaching: Selected articles on writing and teaching.* Upper Montclair, NJ: Boynton/Cook.

National Assessment of Educational Programs. (1998.) *Writing framework and specifications.* National Center for Education Statistics. (2002). NAEP writing results. Retrieved March 18, 2004, from http://www.nces.ed.gov/reportcard/writing/results2002.

National Commission on Writing in America's Schools and Colleges. (2003). The neglected "R": The need for a writing revolution.Retrieved March 18, 2004, from http://www.writingcommission.org.

National Writing Project, & Nagin, C. (2003). *Because writing matters: Improving student writing in our schools.* San Francisco: Josey Bass.

Purves, A., Jordan, S., & J. Peltz. (1996.) *Using portfolios in the English classroom.* Norwood, MA: Christopher-Gordon Publishers.

Resnick, L. B., & Glaser, R. (1976). Problem solving and intelligence. In L.B. Resnick (Ed.), *The nature of intelligence* (pp. 205–230). Hillsdale, NJ: Erlbaum.

Schmidt, P. R. (1996). One teacher's reflections: Implementing multicultural literacy learning. *Equity and Excellence in Education, 29*(2), 20–29.

Schmidt, P. R. (1998). The ABCs of cultural understanding and communication. *Equity and Excellence in Education, 31*((2), 28–38.

Schmidt, P. R. (1999). Know thyself and understand others. *Language Arts, 76*(4), 332–340.

Troutman, D. (1997). Whose voice is it anyway? Marked features in the writing of Black English speakers. In C. Severino, J. C. Guerra, & J. E. Butler (Eds.), *Writing in multicultural settings.* New York: MLA.

Villanueva, V. (1993). *Bootstraps: From an American academic of color.* Urbana, IL: NCTE.

Villanueva, V. (1997). Maybe a colony: And still another critique of the comp community. *JAC: A Journal of Composition Theory, 17*(2), 183–190.

Vygotsky, L. S. (1978). *Mind in society: The development of higher psychological processes.* Cambridge, MA: Harvard University Press.

ACKNOWLEDGMENTS

We are most grateful to all the authors who so generously shared their research, professional insights, and teaching experience by contributing to this book. Our special thanks go to Victor Villanueva and William Thelin, who provided their wise first and last words for the collection. Their perspectives make this book more than a utilitarian handbook of "best practices" in teaching writing or in mentoring teachers. By placing our discussion of gaps amidst larger contexts of literacy practices and writing instruction, a zeitgeist which seems to honor statistics *about* achievement over *real* achievement, a dominant culture which marginalizes the educational needs of people of color and other underrepresented groups, they make this book part of the national discourse on the goals of education and why we must change course. Finally, we gratefully acknowledge Patty Schmidt—our series editor at Information Age Publishing—whose counsel, considerable expertise, and perspective challenged and inspired us.

FOREWORD

Victor Villanueva

One day I turned around and discovered that I had become an old-timer. I had seen the signs: the bags under the eyes that never went away, the salt-and-pepper hair becoming just salt, and grateful for that, as the hair itself disappeared, an expanding forehead, a cheese wheel when I looked at the back of the head, bumps on the joints of fingers, but intellectual life being what it is, I still look to get started in serious reading and writing, still look to do work with meaning, still looking ahead. *Closing the Gap* had me look back, though, at reminders of meanings made.

I

The young man, still sporting long hair and a beard longer than distinguished, walked into the suburban high school in the country's heartland (to conduct a teacher's in-service workshop). It hadn't occurred to him that it was his first time in such a place, that he had never before known this audience before whom he was to act as some sort of authority. But he knew that he was enamored of ideas about literacy, about the notion that folks acquired grammar biologically, with linguists describing what occurred, and that what occurred was sometimes at some distance from the grammar that teachers called "grammar." And the research said, time and again, that the teaching of grammar was not the teaching of writing. He believed that. The research said so. So he said so—with bravado. And they looked at him, the teachers, with looks of patience and kindness.

And he knew—he was told—that these teachers knew little about the teaching of writing and its antecedents in the ancient arts of rhetoric, that it was a new idea, this shift in focus from a kind of literary criticism of what students had written to a focus on how students write, and that the very

Closing the Gap, pages xix–xxii
Copyright © 2007 by Information Age Publishing

process itself was epistemological, a "mode of thinking," some would say, a "mode of discovery," others would say, discovering what had been running around disjointedly in the mind, forced into order by the very linearity of written discourse.

And so he walked in, scared and cocky, equipped with his knowledge, into an environment he had not considered that he didn't know. Green boards and bubble letters cut out of construction paper; words like "anticipatory sets" permanently inscribed on the green board; bright florescent lights; clean, gray metal and light wood, desks free from carved initials, hearts, and obscenities. Foreign. Yet in his arrogance, he hadn't realized how foreign. And as he looked at the sea of teachers' faces, they who looked at him with that kind of love that teachers have for the intellectually engaged (but which he misread as passivity, since they were clearly not awed with his knowledge), looked and carried on about it all, about grammars and dialects and processes, blindly. Blind, he was. And not knowing he was. He didn't want to face that he had not known teachers, neither as colleagues nor as teachers. He was Dr. Dropout, well educated in foundry and carpentry during high-school years, his literacy a product of elementary-school days, of being a sickly kid who read to pass the time away in days when there were only three TV stations, TV itself a later development in his childhood. It hadn't occurred to him that there was learning that could come from these high-school teachers. He would speak of Kenneth Burke and Suzanne Langer and Wolfgang Iser and Lev Vygotsky and Paulo Freire, of Ann Berthoff and Patrick Hartwell and of Flower and Hayes. And it would be they who would learn, he insisted.

Then came the uncomfortable questions, questions about practical applications, about what all this talk of theory and research has to do with the reality of two hundred students a day, of multiple requirements to teach each day, of curricula imposed from above, of student resistance, of survival of those "straddled" with the "nonstandard," of the need to know the conventions of editing, the stuff of grammar. And the gap between my theory and their practice loomed like the Grand Canyon. So unable to bridge the gap, unable to answer and unwilling to divulge ignorance of such matters, the young man resorted to bluster and defensiveness about distances between the insights from the universities and acceptance from "the schools." Not false, acknowledging the gap. But not helpful.

II

A middle-school teacher, calm, reflective, insightful, is assigned (or did he volunteer?) to co-direct the writing project with the young man who would be a professor (was one, a professor, according to job description, but title and reality would take a while to coalesce; that would take a couple of decades more). And then I learned, learned the sense of teachers teaching teachers. Teachers themselves as the bridge across the gap. I watched as Mr. L turned the classroom of teachers into a classroom of students, not students who would hear pronouncements about epistemologies and processes, but a classroom that undergoes those processes, the mode of discovery becoming not only the discovery of those epistemologies, but the teachers discovering what the young man had been carrying on about, discovering their own ways as writers, discovering the intellectual power to be had in writing, discovering the discovery process, and discovering how to work within imposed curricula so as to develop critical consciousness.

And among those teachers in that writing project is one who worked within a school within a school, a teacher of students who had been all but discarded, the remedial, the at risk, the troublemakers, the labeled for failure: the inner city victims of funding allocated on the basis of real estate tax, speakers of dialects I had known as a child, or similar, at least. The young man, me, I watched, watched and learned, learned that what I knew of dialects and code switching really could be put into practice, watched as Mr. T turned students into interpreters, kindly, gently asking students to break it down, the "it" being whatever it was they were saying, to break it down for *him*, to tell him what they were saying and to tell him in ways that would educate him—not "say that in English" but "teach me your ways, since I'm the minority here," students themselves closing the gap, as they educated the white guy in the ways of African American Language, in the differences between a Vietnamese and a Spanish way of seeing and an American English way of seeing, so that in the teaching, they're teaching of him, they learned, learned to be conscious of code switching. And the theory I had espoused on that first day in that suburban school in the heartland about "metalinguistic awareness" took on meaning. Later, I played with those same sets of ideas. Later, I developed so much from all that I had learned from those teachers.

III

I like the word *praxis*. It's not just an affectation for "practice." It is the bringing together of theory and practice. It is the word that speaks of the gap closed. Praxis is at the heart of this volume. This book demonstrates what the young man a couple of decades back had to learn: that there is nothing inherently superior to higher education when it comes to literacy, that theory and research just provide different pieces of the puzzle, that if literacy is going to matter, we have to work together, those of us in the universities and in the schools, have to take the time allotted to some to learn theory and to conduct research and work with those whose time is spent with students by the score.

Eventually, over time, and having ventured off into other matters, the lessons learned a couple of decades ago became like peat moss, an initial layer within the soil that allowed other ideas to bud and maybe to flower. The work has continued. There are those who have continued to refine what one can know of reading theory and its applications to the secondary-school classroom, what one can learn of writing processes and their connections to critical thinking and to critical consciousness, what one can learn from linguists and apply to literacy instruction for all students, no matter their ways with spoken discourse, their distances from a standardized American English, their distances from the written Edited American English. Old insights become new to those walking fresh into the classroom and are added to by the new, so that we continue to learn from the new discoveries of new teachers, no less than from the theorists and the researchers.

In the pages that follow, the theorists and researchers in the universities, the teacher-researchers, the seasoned teachers, and the newcomers come together to bridge the gap between schools and universities. The insights are here, needing to be passed along, needing to be heard, read, engaged.

Pullman, WA
November 10, 2006

PART I

CLOSING GAPS IN TEACHER PREPARATION

CHAPTER 1

TEACHING WRITING

A Matter of Identity, Disposition, and Standard Practice

Sandra Vavra and Sharon Spencer

ABSTRACT

English Educators and secondary English teachers have contributed to a gap between what new teachers learn about how to teach and what they feel they are allowed to practice in the classroom. To address this gap, we argue that English professionals at the university and in the secondary schools should join together to reframe the discipline's identity; accommodate the "back to basics" critics, but on our terms; and embrace the teaching standards already set by NCTE/IRA.

> *Some people see things as they are and ask, "Why?"*
> *I dream of things that might be and ask, "Why Not?"*

The opening quote, often associated with Robert F. Kennedy's unfulfilled 1968 presidential bid, has important implications for the teaching of writing in our high schools and universities. It suggests an energetic, idealistic vision and a willingness to think beyond conventional thinking and the sta-

Closing the Gap, pages 3–12
Copyright © 2007 by Information Age Publishing
All rights of reproduction in any form reserved.

tus quo. During the same era as Kennedy, seminal thinkers (whose research and theorizing followed the Dartmouth Conference) energetically and idealistically re-imagined the English curriculum. The student-centered, process-oriented, authentic kind of writing espoused over the past four decades by these giants—from Moffett, Elbow, Murray, and Macrorie to Graves, Zinsser, Calkins, and Atwell—challenged the traditional pedagogy that has dominated the teaching of secondary school English since the Committee of Ten published its 1894 *Report*. In that document, the Committee defined the main objectives of English teaching as follows:

1. to enable the pupil to understand the expressed thoughts of others and to give expression to thoughts of his own; and

2. to cultivate a taste for reading, to give the pupil some acquaintance with good literature, and to furnish him with the means of extending that acquaintance (as quoted in Nelms, 2000, p. 50)

So influential has the Committee's definition been that even the dazzling promise of the Dartmouth Conference, so carefully crafted over the past forty years, has not *yet* transformed the secondary school English writing curriculum. However, before we ask "why not," it seems useful to examine "why" we aren't yet where we should be.

It all starts with a divided identity. Nelms suggests that the Committee of Ten's decision to join language study and literature study—an ill-advised compromise intended to create a uniform identity for high school English—resulted in what has become a hundred-years' conundrum for the discipline. He adds that, as a consequence of the Committee's statement of goals, "literature has usually emerged as the master . . . ; communication skills the handmaiden—with all the inequity those gender-laden terms imply" (p. 51). As teacher educators, we see the results of a divided identity (language vs. literature) and a favored strand (literature) as we work with teacher candidates in methods courses, and with student teachers and their on-site teacher educators/cooperating teachers in the schools. In our experience at two universities working with teacher candidates in methods courses, we have learned that teaching writing and grading that writing are the greatest concerns our candidates have as they anticipate entering the profession. These concerns have merit.

When we surveyed a number of universities' English Education programs, we found that candidates, on average, are required to study literature three times more than they are required to study language; even more important, although they write papers, they write them outside of class with little feedback as they develop their ideas. Critical interventions by course instructors and/or peers at the first draft and during early revision stages are often missing. Little to no attention is paid to using examples of student writing as course content to illustrate issues of style and alternative ways to express ideas. A prevailing notion seems to exist that if candidates read enough, they will absorb the style and diction of the masters whose narratives they are reading. With enough reading under their belts, candidates will then naturally begin to create sentences which mimic the rhythm, emphasis, and literary panache of a Fitzgerald or Morrison on their own. This notion continues to exist because many English majors do, on average, write at higher levels of sophistication than many of their peers in other disciplines. However, one's ability to write well does not necessarily translate into the ability to teach others how to write well. And, the ability to write a literary analysis that meets a college professor's tastes (an unvarying diet) does not necessarily translate into a robust ability to write effectively for a range of audiences and purposes. Nor does it equip one to teach others how to do so.

Is it any wonder, then, that English Education candidates find it easier to develop literature-based lesson plans than writing-based plans in our methods courses? Or that they "teach" literature in their practicums far more often than they work with high school students on their writing—often increasing the three-to-one ratio they encountered at the university to the point where practicing writing is nearly eliminated from the curriculum. Yet, in our curriculum steering committees, where required curriculum for English Education candidates is determined, we continue to allow the privileging of literature study over the study of communications (language, writing, and speaking). At the University, then, we are complicit in developing a gap between the composition theory and research-based pedagogy our candidates learn in methods courses and the practice in composing they experience in all their other coursework. Clearly, the privileging of *belles lettres* over the utilitarian act of communicating has consequences for English Education candidates. How can they teach writing, and teach it well, when they have not themselves practiced a variety of ways to do so?

The identity problem continues to plague our candidates after they earn their degree and take charge of a classroom of their own. High school teachers carry on the same debate, asking the same questions about core values, as the professors who taught them. Indeed, this seems to be the lasting impression the university holds in the minds of its graduates—How do we define English as a discipline? What shape should the English curriculum take? Which strategies constitute effective and principled practice? Until we address these issues, at minimum in our own university's curriculum and in our teacher-preparation courses, we are guilty of perpetuating a dilemma that often stymies many of our novices and destroys the resolve of many of our most experienced practitioners in the secondary schools.

A second, equally devastating blow to the teaching of writing grows from the lack of a coherent identity. Simply stated, when a discipline lacks a unifying principle, it subjects itself to political whims and institutional forces. If what English *is* is up for grabs, is it any wonder that the process-oriented, culturally sensitive, student-centered, inquiry-based, constructivist learning inspired by the Dartmouth Conference has invited a formidable conservative counter-reaction from parents, school administrators, school boards, politicians, and an increasingly conservative public which favors the traditional teacher-centered methods they themselves experienced in school and simplistic solutions that can be reduced to sound bites, e.g., *back-to-basics, EOG scores, accountability, phonics?*

Without a unifying philosophy, English teachers are particularly vulnerable to institutional demands that often run counter to educational needs. In most communities, secondary schools serve large student bodies. In an attempt to use tax dollars as efficiently as possible, administrators continually seek ways to simplify, to consolidate, to standardize. With no coherent identity for the discipline, English teachers have little ammunition to fight the urge by administrators to reduce their teaching to following consultant-of-the-year scripted lessons and district-developed pacing guides in order to prepare students to pass standardized tests so that the school and district can be designated by labels such as "school of distinction" and thereby continue the cycle endlessly. The hyperbole may seem harsh, but it paints a picture—perhaps not total reality now, but increasingly certain for the future. Nancie Atwell claims that such "programmed instruction give[s] me apoplexy; they take away teachers' professionalism and turn us into mere technicians or, worse, puppets" (*Lessons*, p. xiv). Fully anticipating this course of events two decades ago, James Moffett predicted our dilemma, implicating teachers along with administrators, in *Student-Centered Language Arts and Reading, K–13: A Handbook for Teachers*:

> Good education is not easy to administer and to assess. So just as neither the university professor nor the school teacher is eager to open up the can of worms in changing *composition* from a placid noun to a squirmy verb, the managerial technocrat abhors untidy subjects because they foul up his "systems" approach to cost accounting. Harmony reigns. (Moffett & Wagner, 1983, p. 20)

Given this rather bleak scenario—which pits one hundred years of tradition, a formidable zeitgeist that favors teaching methods largely antithetical to the principled teaching of writing, and an administrative bias which favors a standardized, simplistic educational environment—how is an English educator to respond? Perhaps we should start with a professional disposition like the one demonstrated in the opening quotation—one that envisions what teaching writing (and, indeed, all the language arts) *ought* to be like; one that is willing to accommodate a degree of "subversiveness" (in the Postman-Weingartner sense of the word) as we work to meet the needs of our students; one that operates under a unifying principle so clearly in our own classrooms that our students and candidates really learn to write, despite countervailing political and institutional forces.

Again, we might turn to Moffett, who reframed the identity issue by envisioning the English classroom as the home of a "universe of discourse":

> Language arts or English should be a kind of intellectual "homeroom," where a student can see the totality of his symbolic life. It is the one place where all forms and contents can be learned in relation to each other—the fictional and actual side by side, comprehension and composition as reverses of each other, spoken and written speech interplaying, language competing with and complementing other media. If the rest of the curriculum is to be divided up mostly by topics, then language arts must be not only the guardian of literature but the patron of general communication process. Students need this intensive but comprehensive focus on symbolization so that they will be generally sophisticated speakers, listeners, readers, and writers in the topical subjects. In this broader sense, the language arts might indeed act as a service course to other courses. (Moffett & Wagner, 1983, p. 21)

Without discounting literature study, he deftly positions language study as the keystone of the discipline. More important, by using a theory of communication to define the purpose of English, he shifts it from a passive to an active pedagogy—which is vital to learning and perfecting the *skills* of (rather than just knowledge about) communicating. With a master stroke, he makes it possible for teachers to see "things that might be" in an English classroom. He then outlines a list of authentic discourses by which "[s]tudents should be able to send and receive effectively in oral and written form":

1. Word Play (riddles, puns, tongue twisters, much poetry)
2. Labels and Captions (language joined with pictures of objects, graphs, maps, and so on)
3. Invented Dialogue (improvisation and scripts)
4. Actual Dialogue (discussion and transcripts)
5. Invented Stories (fiction, fables, tales, much poetry, and so on)
6. True Stories (autobiography, memoir, biography, reportage, journals, and so on)
7. Directions (for how to do and how to make)
8. Information (generalized fact)
9. Ideas (generalized thought)

Since each discourse type presents student writers with its own distinct set of comprehension and composition issues, students are continually challenged to think at high critical levels in an endless variety of ways for a multitude of audiences. His theory and accompanying objectives make it easy for teachers to break the stranglehold of literature on the curriculum; after all, the literary essay fits only in category nine (generalized thought) of Moffett's "authentic discourses" and so should not occupy the majority of writing tasks that it traditionally has in the English classroom.

What should dominate classroom time is the practice of writing in general, not the production of one type of writing in the service of assessing a student's or candidate's understanding of literature. Lest the word "dominate" used above be read pejoratively, let us substitute the word "immerse." Immersion in a writing environment is as important to language skill development in school-aged children as immersion in a language-rich environment is to preschool children. Again, Moffett gives us an analogy to prove the point. Moffett argues that young children learn language all day, all the time, at rates of knowledge acquisition far greater than they will ever achieve any other time in their lives (47). Though we cannot hope to duplicate the initial rate at which children learn language, we can hope to increase their now dismal rate of learning to write effectively if we follow the example and immerse students in a writing-rich environment. However, that immersion should not be in only one kind of writing—the literary analysis essay or the five-paragraph informative essay or the formulaic research paper.

Shifting the focus of attention from literature to writing pays off in important ways. It not only solves the identity problem, but also answers the back-to-basics counter-reaction movement. Who can argue that focusing student attention on learning how to communicate well (both orally and in writing) in a variety of authentic ways is not a worthy endeavor for the discipline? And, ironically, it has sound-bite legitimacy, if that is called for. However, "communicating effectively" as a catch phrase for Moffett's theory and objectives does not hamper the principled, teach-to-student-needs methods we should practice the way terms like "grammar basics" and "hooked on phonics" do. That is because it represents a coherent philosophy and accommodates all the research-based pedagogy the Dartmouth Conference inspired. And what could be more "accountable" in our Information Age than working with students and candidates to perfect their ability to write and speak in ever more sophisticated ways? Who can logically argue against the premise that focusing on learning *how* to communicate effectively is worthy of occupying the majority of time in the English classroom, particularly if our ultimate aim is to fully prepare our learners to compete in the global economy? Renowned journalist William Raspberry, who addressed our student body at an Honors Convocation a few years ago, summed up the benefits of learning how to communicate well as follows: "Good English, well spoken and well written, will open more doors for you than a college degree. Bad English will slam doors that you don't even know exist" (Keynote Speech, 2002). In *Writing to Learn*, William Zinsser (1989) frames the issue this way: "Contrary to general belief, writing isn't something that only writers do; Writing is a basic skill for getting through life. Yet most American adults are terrified of the prospect.... Writing is thinking on paper. Anyone who thinks clearly should be able to write clearly—about any subject at all (pp. 10–11).

Once we solve the split-identity problem and position teaching how to communicate effectively as the main work of the English classroom, we are ready to tackle the problem of the institutional bias toward standardization and simplification. It is here where we turn to the process-model researchers and practitioners (including Graves, Murray, Calkins, The Bay Area Writing Project), with special attention to Atwell's workshop approach. The workshop, particularly the post-process model Atwell has developed since she first shared her pedagogy with us in *In the Middle...* (1998), provides a blueprint we can adapt to our own classrooms. It does involve a shift in the way work is done within the English classroom—from a largely teacher-directed, whole group discussion-of-literature followed by individual analytical writing about the literature to a more process-driven, conference-oriented, variety-rich communications environment for multiple audiences and purposes. However, once the initial set-up is completed, the workshop approach provides the ideal environment for encouraging students to develop all their communications (a.k.a. language arts) skills. Atwell (2002) reframes the issue of "simplicity" in *Lessons That Change Writers*:

> The longer I teach, the simpler my teaching becomes. I don't mean that what I ask of kids is simplistic or watered down ... I mean my thinking about teaching has grown less cluttered.... Time and experience have given me twin gifts as a teacher. I know what I can expect from my student writers, and I understand how to help them make good on my expectations.... The clutter of received theories and confused pedagogies has been replaced by a bracing sense of efficiency and productivity, qualities that, as a novice, I never thought to associate with good teaching. (ix)

And so, we are ready to begin asking the "why nots." Or, perhaps, to ask them as "what ifs." What if teacher educators at the university reexamined their curriculums with an eye toward ridding them of the bias toward literature study? What if they altered the focus from literature to writing—not just the *study* of it, but the practice of it? What if these educators re-imagined their methods courses so that students and candidates learned content by means of writing and speaking (and their language arts complements—reading, listening, and viewing) in the variety of modes which occupy Moffett's *universe of discourse*? What if, after grounding our candidates in learning about how to teach writing by directly experiencing it as student writers, teacher educators at the universities were to help candidates sustain long-term professional development through ongoing coaching while novice teachers work through their early years in charge of their own classrooms?

Surely, the current adversaries to many of the research-based teaching practices for writing which the Dartmouth Conference inspired have already begun to focus on writing, by requiring more and more high-stakes, standardized tests of writing achievement (the latest of which is the SAT). Based on her experience in a former life as a training director for a bank, Sandy knows first-hand what characteristics business and industry seek in employees at all levels. At the top of the list is the ability to speak articulately and write with precision. No wonder business leaders are on the back-to-basics bandwagon. While they are equipped to train employees about the business, they are not equipped nor are they interested in taking on the task of teaching employees how to use the language effectively.

Therefore, rather than waste energy by bemoaning or fighting the standardized test issue, why not see the increased focus on writing as an opportunity for English teachers (both in the universities and in the secondary schools) to finally join with adversaries (be they politicians or school boards or an unwitting public just searching for ways to ensure that students really learn important life skills)? Once we cease being adversaries, we may have a freer hand to create the kind of learning environment that students and candidates need in order to gain mastery in written and oral communication.

We teacher educators can also alert our pre-service teachers and remind the on-site teachers educators who mentor them in the secondary schools that, despite our split identity and the conservative zeitgeist which often fails to understand Dartmouth-inspired pedagogy, the NCTE and IRA have jointly managed to create professional standards for curriculum development which heavily favor the teaching of writing (with ten of the twelve standards focused on composing and using language for a variety of purposes, and only two devoted to the study of literature). The standards are as follows:

1. Students read a wide range of print and nonprint texts to build an understanding of texts, of themselves, and of the cultures of the United States and the world; to acquire new information; to respond to the needs and demands of society and the workplace; and for personal fulfillment. Among these texts are fiction and nonfiction, classic and contemporary works.

2. Students read a wide range of literature from many periods in many genres to build an understanding of the many dimensions (e.g., philosophical, ethical, aesthetic) of human experience.

3. *Students apply a wide range of strategies to comprehend, interpret, evaluate, and appreciate texts. They draw on their prior experience, their interactions with other readers and writers, their knowledge of word meaning and of other texts, their word identification strategies, and their understanding of textual features (e.g., sound-letter correspondence, sentence structure, context, graphics).*

4. *Students adjust their use of spoken, written, and visual language (e.g., conventions, style, vocabulary) to communicate effectively with a variety of audiences for a variety of purposes.*

5. *Students employ a wide range of strategies as they write and use different writing process elements appropriately to communicate with different audiences for a variety of purposes.*

6. *Students apply knowledge of language structures, language conventions (e.g., spelling and punctuation), media techniques, figurative language, and genre to create, critique, and discuss print and nonprint texts.*

7. *Students conduct research on issues and interests by generating ideas and questions, and by posing problems. They gather, evaluate, and synthesize data from a variety of sources (e.g., print and nonprint texts, artifacts, people) to communicate their discoveries in ways that suit their purpose and audience.*

8. *Students use a variety of technological and information sources (e.g., libraries, databases, computer networks, video) to gather and synthesize information and to create and communicate knowledge.*

9. *Students develop an understanding of and respect for diversity in language use, patterns, and dialects across cultures, ethnic groups, geographic regions, and social roles.*

10. *Students whose first language is not English make use of their first language to develop competency in the English language and to develop understanding of content across the curriculum.*

11. *Students participate as knowledgeable, reflective, creative, and critical members of a variety of literacy communities.*

12. *Students use spoken, written, and visual language to accomplish their own purposes (e.g., for learning, enjoyment, persuasion, and the exchange of information).* (NCTE/IRA Standards, 1996; emphasis added)

So, the impetus toward writing and language use is already in place. We have only to seize the day.

If the work of seminal thinkers in writing pedagogy has not yet been realized, it seems up to those of us who have followed them to finally make their "dreams" a reality. Perhaps that is the niche we will carve out for ourselves in the history of the discipline. Just as Piaget required a Bruner to translate revolutionary ideas about child development into methods of practical application, so too do the innovators who grew from the Dartmouth Conference's promise require us to finally do the equally important work of "making the intangible tangible, so that every student might know the joy of writing well" (Atwell, 2002, p. xiv). By doing so, we will also be providing a culturally relevant pedagogy for our student writers, as they learn to think critically and communicate clearly about ideas and issues that are important to their personal identity and important to the communities with which they identify (Danielewicz, 2001).

To borrow a bit from our peers in the sciences, we need to turn "why" questions into "what" and "how" questions. We need to ask in *what* ways we can integrate Dartmouth's revolutionary ideas into manageable writing instruction programs and *how* we can help secondary school teachers—bogged down by the requirements imposed by externally imposed *accountability*—to be accountable in ways which meet educational needs (rather than political or institutional ones) and to follow the standards of practice (NCTE/IRA) our profession already has in place. And so we ask, "Why not?"

REFERENCES

Atwell, N. (2002). *Lessons that change writers.* Portsmouth, NH: Heinemann.

Atwell, N. (1998). *In the middle: New understandings about writing, reading, and learning* (2nd ed). Portsmouth, NH: Heinemann.

Danielewicz, J. (2001). *Teaching selves: Identity, pedagogy, and teacher education.* Albany: State University of New York Press.

Moffett, J., & B.J. Wagner. (1983). *Student-centered language arts and reading, K–13: A handbook for teachers* (3rd ed). Boston: Houghton Mifflin Company.

National Council of Teachers of English & International Reading Association. (1996). *Standards for the English language arts.* Urbana, IL & Newark, DE: Author.

National Writing Project. (2003). *Because writing matters: Improving student writing in our schools.* San Francisco: Jossey-Bass.

Nelms, B.F. (2000). Reconstructing English: From the 1890s to the 1990s and beyond. *English Journal, 89*(3), 49–59.

Postman, N., & C. Weingartner. (1969). *Teaching as a subversive activity.* New York: Dell Publishing.

Raspberry, W. (2002, May). Keynote address presented at the Honors' Convocation at North Carolina Central University, Durham, NC.

Zinsser, W. (1989). *Writing to learn.* New York: Harper & Row Publishers.

CHAPTER 2

REFLECTIVE WRITING

Transforming Lives, Ideas, and the Future of English Education

Arlette Ingram Willis and Catherine D. Hunter

ABSTRACT

Given the national increase in culturally and linguistically diverse public school students, there is a gap between what teachers and students bring to the English classroom. The lack of cultural and linguistic familiarity is exacerbated when students who have traditionally been underserved by education in the United States are required to write in Standard Written English used in local, state, and national standards. Drawing inspiration from Toni Morrison's writings, we note that when confronted with teaching writing, the differences between races, ethnicities, cultures, genders, sexual orientations, social classes, languages, beliefs, values, experiences, and worldviews of new teachers and their students can be reconciled by focusing on issues of social justice, equity, and democracy.

Closing the Gap, pages 13–27
Copyright © 2007 by Information Age Publishing
All rights of reproduction in any form reserved.

Be it grand or slender, burrowing, blasting, or refusing to sanctify; whether it laughs out loud or is a cry without an alphabet, the choice word, the chosen silence, unmolested language surges toward knowledge not its destruction.

—Toni Morrison (Nobel Prize Lecture, 1993)

The usual candidates in our English methods classes are white, upper-to-middle class, mono-Standard English speakers, and heterosexual. These collective markers are not meant to deny the many varied experiences of these candidates, but do serve as a point of reference for explaining the gap many experience when confronted with teaching writing to students whose cultural and linguistic understandings, beliefs, and experiences differ from their own. The lack of cultural and linguistic familiarity is exacerbated when students who have traditionally been underserved by education in the United States—students who live in poverty, students of color, students whose first language is not English or Standard American English, and students who are immigrants to this country (hereafter referenced as the underserved)—are required to write in Standard Written English used in local, state, and national standards. Given the national increase in culturally and linguistically diverse public school students, there is a gap between what candidates and students bring to the English classroom. When confronted with teaching writing, the differences between races, ethnicities, cultures, genders, sexual orientations, social classes, languages, beliefs, experiences, and worldviews of new teachers and their students is most apparent.

In framing this chapter we draw upon the celebrated writing and thinking of Toni Morrison, especially her thoughts on the power of language. Like Morrison (1970) we believe understanding *why* should always precede understanding *how*. We offer an explanation for why we have structured the writing portion of our course to center on issues of social justice, equity, and democracy. We also describe how we have transformed our beliefs about the importance of recognizing, accepting, and valuing the humanity of each individual student who enters your classroom and how that respectful stance can influence how writing is taught and evaluated. Further, we explain that our translation and demonstration of theory into practice permits candidates to write/rewrite their world while simultaneously modeling how the process can be used with their future students. Finally, we share examples from our course that illustrate the significance of beginning a writing/rewriting process for social justice and equity with candidates and how their understandings of the process can be translated into high school classrooms.

WRITE YOURSELF INTO THIS SPACE

The vitality of language lies in its ability to limn the actual, imagined and possible lives of its speakers, readers, writers. Although its poise is sometimes in displacing experience it is not a substitute for it.

——Toni Morrison (Nobel Prize Lecture, 1993)

Several years ago while participating in a writer's workshop at Bard College, one of the facilitators began with the prompt, "Write yourself into this space." The idea of naming the space you occupy was an idea we have incorporated into our classes—but we are getting ahead of ourselves because the prompt takes us too far into the course. Let's back up and rewrite ourselves in this space.

OUR THEORETICAL/CONCEPTUAL SPACE

We draw upon Freire's notion of critical literacy and pedagogy where he observes "The reading and writing of the word would always imply a more critical rereading of the world as a 'route' to the 'rewriting—the transformation— of the world" (Freire, 1995, p. 42). Hillocks (1995) in his landmark text *Teaching Writing as Reflective Practice* expressed a similar idea: "writing lies at the heart of education" (p. 212). He expands his thinking on the role of writing in the curriculum, noting: "Each writing experience, to some extent, provides an opportunity to reinvent the self. With each writing, we review our knowledge. In doing so, we have an opportunity to rethink, realign, and reintegrate it, a process that, in effect, changes who we are" (p. 212). In keeping with Freire and Hillocks, we have strategically placed writing assignments throughout the course to encourage authenticity, creativity, and exploration through writing, sharing, performance, and reflection.

Our approach to creating a community of inquiry and praxis is two pronged. First, we have organized the curriculum "around principles of intellectual enrichment, social justice, social betterment, and equity" (Ladson-Billings & Donnor, 2005, p. 295). We help candidates learn to articulate the relationship among theory, research, and practice. We define literacy broadly to include communication between and among co-learners/teachers. This approach helps us to move notions of literacy and communication beyond the academy and socially constructed notions of teaching English/Language Arts toward a moral imperative. Second, along with Kincheloe and McLaren (2005) we argue that teaching "is not unrelated to practices of race, class, and gender oppression but rather intimately related to connect them" (p. 306). In this way we hope to build a more socially just nation of literacy users who advocate for democratic change in how literacy is conceptualized, researched, and taught.

In what we call a series of mini-units, candidates begin to transition from pre-service candidate to teacher. These units include support in (a) building a community of learners/teachers among ourselves; (b) reading, writing, learning about difference through our reading and responding to multicultural/multiethnic and GBLTQ literature; and (c) encouraging and engaging students as a means of preventing classroom management and behavior problems. In addition our syllabus builds and nurtures a classroom that is a supportive community of co-learners/teachers who read, write, and discuss multicultural and multiethnic literature for adolescents.

We believe that self-perception is pivotal in helping candidates better understand themselves as learners/teachers and imperative for teachers in a diverse society. In the first mini-unit candidates learn how to create a sense of community, specifically a learning/caring community of teachers/learners. We begin with self-exploration of what it means to be a person in a racialized society. Then, we share two specific strategies that help to create a collective memory among our candidates, rewriting the world and rewriting the word. We explore what this means—more closely and for some more publicly than ever before—in an autobiographical mini-unit. Our second mini-unit serves as a bridge that spans between the candidate-as-university student to the candidate-as-student teacher. In this mini-unit we read and discuss theories of literacy for high school students that are drawn from classic and contemporary studies in English/Language Arts. We also read, discuss, and demonstrate multiple strategies crafted to engage student writing, including but not limited to the use of grammar as a tool and the rules that accompany its use. Throughout this period of the semester candidates are journaling, completing in-class assignments, creating grammar PowerPoint lessons, sharing their thoughts on electronic WebBoards, and conducting interviews with classroom teachers and high school students. Moreover, candidates complete this mini-unit as they also complete a five-week sojourn in local public high schools as observers and participant observers in English classrooms complete with fieldnotes, a lesson plan, teaching a lesson, and a reflection. While in many ways the lesson plan is typical of those created in most programs—with objectives, procedures, teacher resources, and connections to State or national English standards, we also require candidates to include accommodations in their lessons and assessments for special needs students, students who do not speak English as their first or dominant language, and students whose dialect is not standard/academic. Collectively, these strategies help demonstrate to our candidates how communicative experiences can enhance the teaching of reading and writing to produce new knowledge by inviting students to share their thinking and writing with one another and encourage a more democratic literacy agenda.

ON TEACHING WRITING

Several key concepts anchor our teaching of writing. First, we firmly believe that in order to teach someone to write you must begin by understanding yourself and all that you bring to teaching. Second, as Anne Lamont (1995) reminds us, to write you must be willing to pay attention to the world around you, to relationships and to language with the awe of a child. Third and equally important, is accepting the other person (student writer) as an equal (p. 99). Toni Morrison (1993) captures these ideas in her Nobel Prize speech:

> There is a certain kind of peace that is not merely the absence of war. It is larger than that, ... The peace I am thinking of is the dance of an open mind when it engages another equally open one—an activity that occurs most naturally, most often in the reading/writing world we live in.

We believe that schools, in particular English classrooms where reading and writing occur, should be spaces and places that allow students to experience the peace Morrison describes. We draw upon other ideas about teaching writing from Delpit and Dowdy's (2001) text *The Skin We Speak*. According to the editors, it is important to (a) give each student permission to write, (b) allow students to write about their life experiences in their own language, (c) plan to write daily, and (d) teach Standard Written English for multiple purposes.

OUR LITERAL SPACE

On the first class meeting day of English Language Arts methods, candidates are all abuzz with stories of how they spent their summer, who got engaged, who broke up, and scores of plans for the semester and beyond. The professor and teaching assistant enter the room and voices begin to soften, conversations begin to cease. Introductions are made and icebreakers are exchanged. Then the syllabus is distributed to candidates. A hush hovers over the room—syncopated by an occasional gasp, cough, and turning of the pages—before eyes glaze over as we read through the multi-page syllabus printed on neon-bright paper. Reading through the syllabus, followed by questions and answers, usually ends the first class session. Candidates often express surprise because of the sheer volume of work and the high level of expectations outlined in the syllabus. Most are overwhelmed by the number of texts that are required reading: theory, research, and professional articles as well as fiction, nonfiction, and plays. They are unaware that the scholarship and craftsmanship they will read are dominated by scholars and authors of color. The candidates sense, and rightly so, that this is not the sort of class where their wealth of mainstream or canonical background knowledge will suffice nor the sorority file cache will help. Further, the candidates are aware that they will need to read, write, and learn some things altogether new that are integral to teaching in a diverse society.

Our goal is to prepare English educators to welcome, accept, teach, and reward each child that enters their classrooms. We do not want their idea of teaching to be limited to someone else's idea of 'best practices' or to standardized packaged texts and materials. To set the stage for this type of learning, we model the processes within our classroom. Moreover, the syllabus appears to alert the class that they are transitioning from student candidate, to pre-service educator, to educator in the twenty-first century. The syllabus clearly demonstrates that candidates need to be prepared for all their students, but more so for students of color, students whose first language is not English or standard English, students who live in poverty, and students who are recent immigrants to this country. In this first step into their new careers, our candidates learn that they must complete the steps of reading, writing, reflecting, and critiquing the work of scholars and experts in the field and also the ongoing work of their lives, perceptions, prejudices, and beliefs.

Reactions from candidates include questioning the validity of many of the assignments such as the autobiographical poem—to be performed, not merely written or read. After all, they ask, what does this assignment have to do with their development as teachers, methods of teaching, and expertise in the content area of English? The candidates pose legitimate/reasonable/valid concerns; however, their concerns belie preconceived notions about *whose* knowledge, and, *what* knowledge is of worth. Our candidates possess preconceived notions of what should be taught in an English Language Arts methods course that includes lesson planning, grammar, vocabulary, writing, literature, and test preparation. They also tend to believe that there are multiple wrong ways and only one right way to teach, speak, write, and read. Missing from their thinking is self-awareness, values, perceptions, and introspection as well as an understanding that there are multiple ways to teach, speak, write, and read. For candidates who have grown accustomed to learning and offering answers that are reflective of Eurocentric ways of knowing and responding in English Language Arts classrooms, it is difficult to survive the course.

OUR CANDIDATES

Much like other teacher educators nationally we are faced with preparing candidates—who are predominately white, upper-to-middle class, monolingual, and heterosexual females—for secondary classrooms that are growing ever more racially/ethnically and linguistically diverse, economically segregated, and technologically savvy. Many of these candidates write essays for admission that detail their lack of interaction, much less knowledge, of cultures and languages beyond their own. For most of our candidates, a focus on diversity arose in part as they were required to address diversity, or the lack of diversity in their lives, as part of their essay for admission. It is at this point that many admit that they begin to consider people unlike themselves as possible members of a student population that they may teach in the future.

The enrollment for the course averages approximately 25–30 candidates per semester. Although each candidate is unique, several broad composite descriptors of the types of candidates (social justice activist, laissez-faire, passive, and resistant) who enter our classes might be helpful to the reader. First, there are candidates that enter the class with a social activist predisposition; typically, they have read widely, especially critical and post-structural theories. Second, there are candidates who seek to please the professor, although they may or may not buy into the pedagogy and curriculum. Third, there are candidates who seem to have no particular thought when they enter the course other than teaching English. Fourth, there are candidates who resist the instructor, curriculum, pedagogy, and readings. (Naturally, there are points along this continuum not included.) Most of our candidates imply that they have only the best intentions of teaching every student in their class regardless of race, class, gender, first language, immigrant status, or sexual orientation; unfortunately, good intentions are not good enough. Our candidates need to acquire predispositions and attitudes to address inequities inherent within literacy theories and research as well as acquire skills and strategies to improve instruction. To varying degrees, many candidates appear to be propelled by the idea of imitating a former high school English teacher, professor, relative, or coach whom they believe they will replicate. Our candidates desire to infuse the lives of their future students with the experiences they have had—seemingly unaware of a need for change, both in interpersonal communication and English Language Arts education since their high school days.

As profiled in the composites described above, our candidates come to us with static beliefs about what English teachers do and do not do, based in large part on their own high school experiences. These beliefs about teaching English will be later reproduced in the curriculum (Edelsky, Smith, & Wolfe, 2002), if there is no intervention during their professional development. Part of what our course seeks to do is to reorientate candidates (1) to think about education as a lifelong pursuit and (2) to be prepared to teach real students in classrooms, not generic or mythical students who are ever compliant. Real students, especially the Underserved, bring all of who they are to each classroom. Often teachers (both in- and pre-service) are unprepared/underprepared (NCES, 1999) to address the struggles faced by these students. Fine and Weiss (2005) also indicate that Underserved students struggle against the realities imposed by teachers, where they "must theorize their own identities relationally all the time and every day, because they are making selves in spaces where 'difference' matters. That is, they are learning, claiming, and negotiating their places in a microcosmic racial/classed hierarchy on a daily basis" (Fine & Weiss, 2005, p. 75).

We take seriously our responsibility to prepare our candidates for the U.S. public school population that is growing ever more racially, ethnically, and linguistically diverse (Willis, 1997, 1998, 2000). Fortunately, our candidates, fearfully yet wonderfully, respond to the coursework. For many of the candidates it is the first time that they have been asked to be both reflective and critical of not only the work of celebrated canonical authors of the literary world, but also of themselves, their ideas, and their practices as they prepare to take their position as teachers among the nation's diverse population of adolescents and young adults. Painfully, they become aware of the undeniable link between teacher beliefs and perceptions and student academic success.

WRITING/REWRITING THE WORLD:
SELF, POETRY, AND PERFORMANCE

There is really nothing more to say—except why. But since why is difficult to handle, one must take refuge in how.

—Morrison (1970)

The course begins with a mini-autobiographical unit that includes sending an electronic jpg photo; a biopoem; a family tree; writing and sharing an artifact/memory; reading others' personal narratives; and writing and sharing a personal narrative. Additionally, our candidates read and construct an autobiography Webpage from selected titles, and they write and perform an autobiographical poem. We work with candidates to complete the multiple activities associated with the mini-autobiographical unit. Key to this mini-unit is that candidates openly share their life experiences. As Hillocks (1995) observes, "To the extent that ones' self is one's total collection of memories and their relationships to one another, the self that pulls together bits and pieces of experience in ways that they may never have been conjoined before is in the process of becoming a new self" (p. 212).

Candidates' willingness and openness are encouraged, but not forced. We are preparing most of our candidates to teach in public high schools, socially constructed spaces where they will need to be comfortable within themselves as well as their levels of English expertise. Therefore, we extend the notion of writing about self to personal narratives where "writing stories are not about people and cultures "out there . . . rather, they are about ourselves" (Richardson & St. Pierre, 2005, p. 966). We encourage our candidates to include writing personal narratives into their future teaching plans. The importance of personal stories cannot be underestimated, especially for students who feel alienated in schools where their life stories and stories of people whose lives mirror their own are ignored.

The culminating activity (the writing and performance of an autobiographical poem) shifts the focus away from standards and conventions of poetry to the personal, lived experiences of the individual student—similar to what Denzin (2003) describes as critical performance pedagogy. Kincheloe and McLaren (2005) additionally argue that "knowledge must be enacted—understood at the level of human beings' affect and intellect" (p. 315).

This activity is a milestone for the class as well as many individual candidates. The autobiographic poem is written, then performed; however, it is the performance that serves as "a doorway, an instrument of encounter, a place of public and private negotiations—where the goal is not just to empathize, but to attend" (Salverson, quoted in Jones, 2005, p. 772). During this activity we generally see many candidates share their innermost concerns more honestly and publicly than before. We find that the performance of autobiographical poems helps candidates to "expose the hidden, clarify the oblique, and articulate the possible" (Madison, 2005, p. 538). The performances are videotaped, burned onto DVDs, and given to candidates at the end of semester. Madison (2005) writing about her own performance research, but clearly applicable to other uses of performance, notes that performance "offers the alchemy of human connection, conjoinment, and intersubjectivity to the power and ubiquity of memory. We remember how this communication felt for us and for each other, together. It was made even more powerfully human because it was publicly performed" (p. 544).

We envision the autobiographical poem and performance as a writing of our candidates' world into the world of teaching. Or, as Madison (1998) writes, it is an opportunity where the "active, creative work that weaves the life of mind with the being mindful of life, of 'merging text and the world' (p. 277). Writing the poem and performing it is an opportunity for candidates to "look deeply into themselves and their biases and values, precisely

because these are, inadvertently or not, brought to the students they teach"
(Nieto quoted in Franquiz, 2005, p. 170). We join Nieto in our concern
that our candidates understand diversity beyond notions of difference and
make a deep and personal commitment to understanding what they, as
teachers, will bring to their future students. The gap between the understandings and life experiences of many white candidates and their preparation and ability to teach writing to culturally and linguistically diverse
students is best summed in the following excerpt drawn from Senator
Barack Obama's (2004) autobiography. Although he is speaking of college
students' experience, the idea can be seamlessly extended to the experiences of many high school students—in part because he captures the cau-
tions that invade the thinking of students from culturally and linguistically
diverse backgrounds and in part because he pinpoints their fears:

> To admit our doubt and confusion to whites, to open up our psyches to gen-
> eral examination by those who had caused so much of the damage in the first
> place, seemed ludicrous, itself an expression of self-hatred—for there
> seemed no reason to expect that whites would look at our private struggles as
> a mirror into their own souls, rather than yet more evidence of black pathol-
> ogy. (p. 193)

We believe our autobiographical mini-unit is a starting point for our
candidates to begin to write/rewrite their own worlds and to more seriously and honestly begin to acknowledge the necessity for permitting students to write/rewrite their worlds in English classrooms.

REWRITING THE WORD: TRANSACTING
WITH MULTICULTURAL/MULTIETHNIC LITERATURE

Although our candidates have begun the journey of rewriting the world,
we recognized that the mini-autobiography unit is a one-way reflection that
needs to be broadened to reflect the global diversity and diversity within
their classes, or the lack thereof. To address diversity in English/Language
Arts classrooms and to rectify the one-way reflective process we read,
respond, and interrogate multicultural and multiethnic literature. At the
midpoint of the course and in preparation for writing a nine-week unit for
use in secondary schools, candidates read ten works (autobiography/mem-
oir, plays, fiction, nonfiction, collections of short stories) that include
canonical and contemporary titles (five are selected by the instructor and
five are selected by the students). The titles are used for demonstration lessons, lesson and unit planning, and literature discussions. What we find
most informative about these readings are the responses written by our

candidates as they transact (Rosenblatt, 1995) with text written outside of their experiences and comfort levels.

Through reading and writing reflections on a variety of works written by scholars and authors of color, candidates begin to understand more clearly that teaching English is political and biased; it is not nor has it ever been, neutral. They also begin to acknowledge and address the Eurocentrism in the canon that has been foisted upon all students irrespective of the rhetoric of universalism, Americanism, or tradition. Put another way, this literature also helps to "democratize the representational sphere of culture by locating the particular experiences of individuals in a tension with dominant expressions of discursive power" (Neumann, quoted in Jones, 2005, p. 765). For some candidates the reality is jarring and they react with oral and written statements that reflect the broad composite (homogenous) candidate worldview described at the beginning of this piece:

> **Activist:** Finally, we get to learn something that will be useful.
>
> **Laissez-faire:** I am afraid of making a mistake and offending someone or some group, it's probably better if I don't do anything rather than do something wrong.
>
> **Passive:** This stuff is all good, but I heard that in the suburbs you really don't need to know much about multiculturalism because they don't have many diverse students.
>
> **Resistant:** I went to a school that was 99.9 percent white, and never knew any of this stuff. Do I really need to learn all this multicultural and diversity stuff along with everything else I have to learn in English, and be prepared to teach it too?

There is another popular statement that we hear nearly every semester: "Isn't it better to just have multicultural literature be a part of the curriculum and not singled out?" Together with candidates we interrogate notions of the canon, authentic text, and insider/outsider perspectives to determine what is valued in the teaching of English, to ask why, and to discuss ways to foster change. In this way, candidates who have begun to understand their roots are being asked to find routes (Hall, 1996) to help their future students become effective readers and writers.

We remind our candidates in multiple ways that differences are social constructions that can be reconstructed, replaced, or abandoned. Madison (2005), speaking specifically of race, put it this way: "race is constructed, reconstructed, and deconstructed depending on locale, history, and power, but immediate experience sometimes penetrates deeper" (p. 541). Drawing on notions of critical theory and pedagogy, candidates are required to link passages in the literature they are reading to historical events, to write in response to a prompt designed to help them interrogate the literature, and to perform in response to their reading using art, music, drama, technology, etc.

In this methods course, much like secondary English classrooms, literature forms the heart of the curriculum. It is usually during candidates' writing that we track shifts and changes in candidates—from icy resistance and resolve not to change, to more open-minded understanding of the need for change. In our teaching it appears that reading literature written by a racially/ethnically and linguistically diverse group of authors; responding to the literature in written, oral, and performance formats; and discussing the literature within our community of learners forces students to move outside of any voyeurism of the past and to actively engage with the text, characters, stories, lived experiences, and one another. The resistant candidates find this mini-unit most difficult when they retreat to their comfort level—e.g., seeking errors in craft (character formation, tone, style, pace), mechanics, conventions, etc.—while simultaneously refusing to engage with the text, characters, stories, and histories that surround the text.

Candidates of all ilks find these activities unnerving, especially those who have been taught there is one right answer, that there is one way of seeing and perceiving text, that there is one interpretation of text and life, and that they have been rewarded for being in accordance with the reproduction of the status quo. We do not use multicultural and multiethnic literature merely to point out the differences between cultures, cultural ways of knowing, or nuances among cultures. We use multicultural and multiethnic literature (both in reading and writing) to illustrate that it can be used in all classrooms to encourage social justice and equity.

CONCLUSION

Sexist language, racist language, theistic language—all are typical of the policing languages of mastery, and cannot, do not permit new knowledge or encourage the mutual exchange of ideas.

—Toni Morrison (Nobel Prize Lecture, 1993)

Although the reactions mentioned at the onset of this chapter typify the beginning of the semester, no one can claim that there is a typical end of the semester or year-long journey upon which the candidates embark in the fall. The syllabus marks a point of departure. The destination is determined by each candidate who decides to, or not to, authentically interact with each topic and with peers. The syllabus is a living document that seeks to bring depth and breath to the methodological, pedagogical, theoretical, and experiential development of the candidates. Therefore, the syllabus maintains a core menu of assignments and events but evolves continually to incorporate cutting-edge research and topics of emerging educational, political, and cultural significance. Quite often the evolution of the syllabus is in response to concerns that have been raised by candidates in previous semesters.

Each evolution and revision of the syllabus is designed to facilitate and encourage transformative possibilities for the candidates. With each writing assignment they are challenged gently to reexamine and to perhaps reinvent the self, rethink their thoughts, and de-center that which has always stood front and center. We do, after all, teach for change. The journey is arduous for us all, but the rewards are abundant, particularly for the candidates who opened themselves to difference and to differing points of view. On the last meeting day of the class the candidates are all abuzz as in the beginning. Now they review each other's Professional Portfolio, giggle and gasp about how much their ideas have changed, their writing has changed, and they have changed. The professor and the teaching assistant enter the room and voices begin to soften, conversations begin to cease. Final comments are made and good-byes are exchanged. The portfolios are collected from the candidates and class is dismissed. Whether the candidates entered the course with an activist, laissez faire, passive, or resistant position, we have demonstrated what it means to welcome and accept each person. Many emerge more focused and more committed to teach for change by the end of the year. Candidates who entered the class reluctantly, gasping at the syllabus, now depart reluctantly, uttering shrills of joy at their hard work and accomplishments. Through reflective writing and practice each candidate has, to varying degrees, made a more critical writing of the world in this space.

REFERENCES

Delpit, L., & Dowdy, J. K. (2001). *The skin we speak: Thoughts on language and culture in the classroom.* New York: New Press.

Denzin, N. (2003). *Performance ethnography: Critical pedagogy and the politics of culture.* Thousand Oaks, CA: Sage.

Edelsky, C., Smith, K., & Wolfe, P. (2002). A discourse on academic discourse. *Linguistics and Education 13*(1), 1–38.

Fine, M., & Weis, L. (2005). Compositional studies, in two parts: Critical theorizing and analysis on social (In)justice. In N. Denzin & Y. Lincoln (Eds.), *The sage handbook of qualitative research* (3rd ed., pp. 65–84). Thousand Oaks, CA: Sage.

Franquiz, M. E. (2005). Education as political work: An interview with Soma Nieto. *Language Arts, 83*(2), 166–171.

Freire, P. (1995). *Pedagogy of hope: Reliving pedagogy of the oppressed* (R. Barr, Trans.). New York: Continuum.

Hall, S. (1996). Who needs identity? In S. Hall & P. du Gay (Eds.), *Questions of cultural identity*. London: Sage.

Hill-Collins, P. (2000). *Black feminist thought: Knowledge, consciousness, and the politics of empowerment*. New York: Routledge (originally published in 1990).

Hillocks, G. (1995). *Teaching writing as reflective practice*. New York: Teachers College Press.

Jones, S. (2005). Autoethnography: Making the personal political. In N. Denzin & Y. Lincoln (Eds.), *The Sage handbook of qualitative research* (3rd ed., pp. 763–792). Thousand Oaks, CA: Sage.

Kincheloe, J., & McLaren, P. (2000). Rethinking critical theory and qualitative research. In N. Denzin & Y. Lincoln (Eds.), *The Sage handbook of qualitative research* (2nd ed., pp. 279–314). Thousand Oaks, CA: Sage.

Kincheloe, J., & McLaren, P. (2005). Rethinking critical theory and qualitative research. In N. Denzin & Y. Lincoln (Eds.), *The Sage handbook of qualitative research* (3rd ed., pp. 303–342). Thousand Oaks, CA: Sage.

Ladson-Billings, G., & Donnor, J. (2005). The moral activist role of critical race theory scholarship. In N. Denzin & Y. Lincoln (Eds.), *The Sage handbook of qualitative research* (3rd ed.), (pp.279 - 302). Thousand Oaks, CA: Sage.

Lamont, A. (1995). *Bird by bird: Some instructions on writing and life*. New York: Anchor.

Madison, D. (2005). Critical ethnography as street performance: Reflections of home, race, murder, and justice. In N. Denzin & Y. Lincoln (Eds.), *The Sage handbook of qualitative research* (3rd ed., (pp. 537–342). Thousand Oaks, CA: Sage.

Morrison, T. (1993). Nobel Prize Lecture. Available: MACROBUTTON HtmlRes Anchor http://nobelprize.org/literature/laureates/1993/morrison-lecture.html. Retrieved, February 27, 2006.

Morrison, T. (1970). *The bluest eye*. New York: Plume.

National Center for Education Statistics (NCES). (1999). *Teacher quality: A report on the preparation and qualifications of public school teachers*. NCES 1999–080. Washington, DC: U.S. Department of Education.

Neumann, M. (1996). Collecting our selves at the end of the century. In C. Ellis & A. Bochner, (Eds.), *Composing ethnography: Alternative forms of qualitative writing* (pp. 172–198). Walnut Creek, CA: AltaMira.

Obama, B. (2004). *Dreams from my father : A story of race and inheritance*. New York: Three Rivers Press.

Richardson, L. & St. Pierre, E. (2005). Writing: A method of inquiry. In N. Denzin & Y. Lincoln (Eds.), *The Sage handbook of qualitative research* (3rd ed., pp. 959–978). Thousand Oaks, CA: Sage.

Rosenblatt, L. (1995). *Literature as exploration*. New York: Modern Language Association. (original work published 1938).

Salverson, J. (2001). Change on whose terms? Testimony and an erotics of inquiry. *Theater, 31*(3), 119–125.

Willis, A. I. (2000). Keeping it real: Learning about culture, literacy, and respect. *English Education, 32*(4), 267–277.

Willis, A. I. (Ed.), (1998). *Teaching multicultural literature in grades 9–12: Moving beyond the canon*. Norwood, MA: Christopher-Gordon.

Willis, A. I. (1997). Exploring multicultural literature as cultural production. In T. Rogers & A. Soter (Eds.), *Reading across cultures: Teaching literature in a diverse society* (pp. 135–160). New York: Teachers College Press.

CHAPTER 3

TEACHER ADVOCACY IN ENGLISH EDUCATION

Amy Goodburn and April Lambert

ABSTRACT

Most English education programs focus on theories of literacy learning without preparing candidates to advocate for why they do what they do in the classroom. To address this gap, we argue that professional development programs should engage candidates in exploring concepts and strategies of advocacy. We believe that equipping candidates with tools for advocacy can better prepare them for the highly political roles that they will inhabit in and outside of the classroom as well as help them to assist students in advocating for their own purposes.

As English educators, we have been—and asked our students to be—active participants in the classroom. We have written back to texts, argued with authors, questioned our own practices, and redefined our own positions and understandings. Why, then, does this sort of activism often stop at the moment of English methods, a critical point when the pre-service student begins to develop his or her teacher identity? In this essay, we suggest that English teacher education can (and must) do more to prepare candidates for the advocacy roles they will inhabit. We believe a primary task in teaching English is to advocate for particular practices, beliefs, and values. Thus,

Closing the Gap, pages 29–41

we argue that the concept of "advocacy," and strategies to engage in advocacy, should be foregrounded in the professional development of secondary English teachers. Beyond preparing high school English teachers to advocate for their students' learning, we suggest that helping teachers name and understand their roles as advocates can also equip them to better prepare high school students to use advocacy in their lives.

There's no question that we know much about what adolescents need to foster their literacy in the secondary classroom (NCTE Guidelines "A Call to Action: What We Know About Adolescent Literacy and Ways to Support Teachers in Meeting Students' Needs"). As teachers, we know that adolescents need student-initiated conversations regarding texts that are authentic and relevant to real life experiences. We know that students need curricula that connect their home and school literacy experiences, that they need opportunities to write for their own purposes and contexts, and that they need to receive ongoing and authentic response to this writing. What we as teachers don't seem well prepared to do, though, is advocate for these practices to students, parents, educational policy makers, and sometimes even our own colleagues. Despite the fact that we find ourselves daily having to rationalize and advocate for why we do what we do, there is little discussion of how best to prepare us for these roles. While current literature focuses on identity as a central starting point for teacher development, there is little discussion of how teacher identity connects to teachers' comfort levels in advocating for pedagogical and curricular choices.

To illustrate why we believe the term "advocacy" should be foregrounded in the intellectual work of preparing secondary English teachers, we first discuss the role of agency in teacher development. We then describe three scenarios that represent different forms of advocacy in which we have found ourselves and that we believe are fairly common to those involved in teaching English/Language Arts. Finally, we outline strategies for examining "advocacy" that can easily be integrated into both pre-service English Education courses and secondary English classrooms. Ultimately, we believe that attending to advocacy in the English classroom empowers teachers to successfully navigate and bridge the gaps between what they believe and know about best practices for language learning and the complex realities of the secondary English classroom.

TEACHER IDENTITY AND AGENCY

A common criticism of teacher development literature in English Education is that it focuses either on scripted approaches or methods that seem unanchored to the realities of secondary school environments. As a result, pre-service candidates are often faced with multiple and oftentimes competing understandings of what English teaching encompasses (Kelly, 2004). Moreover, while the gap between university education and secondary schools is often discussed, our experiences suggest that even within a university teacher education program, pre-service candidates often experience a range of theories and conceptual models for how best to support literacy learning. Indeed, Kelly (2004) suggests that many teacher education programs do not help beginning teachers understand the complexity of the contexts in which they will work: "Pulled in various directions, such a teacher must begin to negotiate and reconcile the expectations of the curriculum, the profession, the teacher education program, and any personal hopes and dreams of what English teaching is, could, or should be" (p. 58). She argues that instead of foregrounding decontextualized methods such as writing workshops or literature circles, we need to conceptualize teacher education as a site for engaging candidates in exploring and probing the tensions they face in understanding teaching as an ethical and political practice.

In a similar vein, Danielewicz (2001) argues in *Teaching Selves* that teacher education needs to focus less on methods and more on how future teachers conceptualize their identities. "What makes someone a good teacher is not methodology, or even ideology," Danielewicz writes. "It requires engagement with identity, the way individuals conceive of themselves so that teaching is a state of being, not merely ways of acting or behaving" (p. 3). This notion of identity as critical to teacher education is further supported by Ritchie and Wilson's (2000) research in *Teacher Narrative as Critical Inquiry: Rewriting the Script.* Based on their findings of a multi-year qualitative study that tracked pre-service teachers through their teaching careers, they argue that candidates need to understand the cultural, political, and social scripts that shape their understandings of what teachers are and should be. April's reflections on her experiences echo these researchers' views that imagining a teacher identity is central:

> As a high school student, I hated English class, and I continued to deny a voice inside of me that pleaded to be a teacher. After all, how could I teach high school English if I despised it so much? It was only my pure love of reading that sustained me through what I considered to be the work of English. While my teacher led us through *Hamlet* and *The Grapes of Wrath,* I read Dreiser's *An American Tragedy,* Rand's *The Fountainhead,* and Steinbeck's *East of Eden.* To an outsider, my personal reading might have looked no different from the texts studied in my English classroom. However, my own reading had everything to do with my identity and interests. In my own mind I could make personal connections to the characters, plots, or ideas of these novels, creating a sort of conversation of connections that was not made available in my English classroom. At the time, I could not articulate the distinction between my personal joy in reading and the suffering I experienced in

English class. Instead of being an active participant, I felt like an oppressed prisoner in an English classroom jail cell. Clearly, I had no desire to fulfill the role of "English teacher" that I had come to know.

Once I entered the field of collegiate English, I found discussions of identity and argument all around me. In fact, I felt a sense of agency that encouraged and engaged me to pursue specific studies. There was finally a place for my identity as I engaged in reading and writing projects that took up my own history, questions, and ideas. My identity continued to flex and fluctuate as I began to realize that my love for English could be translated into a new kind of teacher identity. I found myself becoming an advocate for the kind of English I had pursued privately, desperately wanting the affective part of English to find a place in the high school curriculum. I finally had the identity, and through it the professional voice and passionate agency, to affect and impact the field of secondary English education.

What April's reflections and teacher development literature suggest is that encompassed within our notion of teacher identity is the concept of agency, a sense that one can effectively argue for particular practices, curricula, and environments with a sense of power and authority. It is this sense of agency that we think needs to be made more central in teacher education as a means of helping pre-service candidates successfully advocate for themselves, their students, and their school communities. In this respect, we argue for a view of teacher education in English/Language Arts that parallels what Stenberg and Lee (2002) describe as "a shift away from concepts to be acquired and theories to be mastered and toward ongoing, locally specific dialogue between teaching and research, action and reflection" (p. 345). In short, how can we help English teachers imagine themselves as powerful advocates for rather than technicians of particular pedagogical approaches, curricula, and teaching practices?

To illustrate what we mean by "advocacy," we present three scenarios that show how students and teachers are often called upon to advocate in the English classroom. These scenarios are drawn from April's experiences, first as a high school student, then as a pre-service English Education candidate, and finally as a student teacher in a secondary classroom. While April may not have fully realized her goals as an advocate in these scenarios, reflecting upon them demonstrates a definite and powerful need for theorizing the role that advocacy plays in teachers' and students' lives.

HIGH SCHOOL STUDENT ADVOCACY

As a junior in high school, I witnessed an incredible form of student-led advocacy. My small parochial school was in the process of "weeding out" its library. As a result, mounds of books found their way to the dumpster. While some of the books were rotting and merited disposal, most were in fine condition; they had simply been left on the library shelves too long. Upon discovering the book-filled dumpster, several of my classmates took the initiative to save them by depositing them in the back of one student's Isuzu Trooper. Angered that the books had been removed and disposed of so covertly, they believed that a better option would have been to offer the books to the community or, at the very least, recycle them.

A few days later, a miniature version of an underground school newspaper surfaced. Creatively dubbed "Trash or Treasure?" this newspaper advocated for a less covert and more practical approach to the library thinning. The newspaper itself was a complex literacy piece with a well-defined argument and intricate language. I stood in awe of my classmates for what they had done—not led by any adult or teacher, they had taken the initiative to speak out for their beliefs. However, all of the students quickly learned the result of being an advocate: a week of in-school suspension. The administration's response sent an obvious message to students and teachers about their unwillingness to consider any type of advocacy or argument, no matter how well founded. I think back to that moment as a critical point in my own feelings about advocacy because as a result of the incident, I was forced to think about advocacy strategies, and the consequences of those strategies, at a very young age.

We profile this example of high school student advocacy because the response of the school administration represents what many in English Education have noted as the norm. As Beck (2005) notes, teaching students to be critical questioners of school practices and policies "is not without risks to students, teachers, and the institutions in which they are embedded" (p. 392). In this case, the school administrators felt threatened and sought to deliberately curtail the act without examining its purpose or value. While we can read the newsletter as an elevated literacy act—the students had a definite purpose and audience and wrote in a skillful and effective way that reached students and parents—we can also read this moment as a pointer to the dangers of student advocacy. The students' suspension illustrates the complexities involved in helping students advocate on their own behalf. But we also note this example of advocacy because it represents a classroom experience that has profoundly shaped April's understanding of what advocacy can mean in the classroom, both as a student and as a pre-service candidate. Regardless of whether she supported her classmates' actions, she was taught a powerful message about the right of students to voice their perspectives and to advocate their positions. This advocacy moment is an important part of her educational history and contributes to her evolving understanding of "agency" in relation to teacher identity, of the ways that she might advocate for and with students. April's memory of this advocacy moment is important, then, in terms of the weight it carries into her present and future teaching identity. Since most teacher education programs do not ask candidates to explore their histories with advocacy, April's opportunity to theorize the gap between her experiences as a high school student and her future role as a teacher would be lost.

The second scenario represents a moment when April, in combination with her pre-service candidate cohort, advocated for the conditions of her own learning in light of the theories she had learned about English teaching. By this time, April's teacher identity was more willing to become a direct participant in the advocacy process.

PRE-SERVICE TEACHER ADVOCACY

In the first two semesters of my English Education courses, we debated the value of grammar in the English classroom within the context of whole language or writing workshop approaches. We discussed social contexts and the social differences that may or may not divide us from our future students. And in our writing courses, we were encouraged to experiment with multi-genre writing formats as opposed to traditional five-paragraph essays. In these courses, we learned to be critical educators, engaging in self-questioning in order to theorize our approaches to the English classroom. While my pre-service class members and I had differing values about English based on these courses, we were all prepared to critique, analyze, probe, and, ultimately, defend what we valued about the teaching of English.

However, a stark reality hit my peers in a later semester when our new methods instructor evaluated our first article response not for its content, but for its grammar. In fact, this instructor who had been charged to guide us in our development as English teachers looked solely at the grammatical aspect of our response without any regard for what we were saying or arguing for. In our previous classes, we had come to value the critical questioning our instructors spurred in the margins of our papers, asking, "Why do you believe this?" or "What will this look like in your classroom?" Now we were faced with lessons on how not to split infinitives or the rules for comma placement. Ironically, many of these "grammar lessons" had been debated hotly and denounced in our prior methods classes. When our instructor's response to our lesson plans remained grammar-based (with no opportunity for critical reflection or thought) we took a stand.

The critical engagement that we had become so accustomed to in our methods courses soon moved outside the classroom as we huddled in the hallway to discuss our frustrations and reaffirm one another's beliefs. E-mails zoomed from inbox to inbox as my peers and I developed arguments and proposals for action. In class, we confronted our instructor, advocating for more critical responses to our lesson plans. When this prompted no change, we took our concerns to other department faculty who also advocated for a curriculum that addressed critical aspects of teacher education. As a final measure, half of the pre-service students met with the Dean of Teachers College to discuss the disjunction between our previous courses and the current one. Desperately advocating for our own education, we were finally able to show our college administrators the fragmentation that was occurring in our department. Even though we were the sacrificial lambs, we came away from that semester knowing that things would improve for future methods students. It remains surprising to my classmates and me, though, how quickly and unpredictably we were pressed to become advocates for our own education.

In this scenario, April and her cohort of pre-service candidates faced a dilemma when competing paradigms for literacy learning were being taught within her pre-service program. The gap between what April and her cohorts believed to be true about English language methods and their experiences within the methods course created dissonance that required the candidates to strategize how to advocate for their learning. While April noted that this advocacy moment required both intellectual and emotional resources that couldn't have been "taught" through any kind of rehearsals, she also noted that the prior methods courses had equipped her and her classmates to become powerful advocates because they were asked to systematically reflect upon their beliefs and rationalize their teaching theories in these settings. In terms of advocacy, these courses were critical for sponsoring April's transformation into becoming what she describes as "an English education advocate."

A key component of this transformation was collaboration and support from peers. For these pre-service candidates, collaborating as a group enabled them to rehearse and revise their beliefs and strategies in a private arena before making them public to the methods teacher, the other faculty, and the Dean of the college. Even though these candidates held differing perspectives on the best strategies and alternatives for what could and should be achieved in English course work, their arguments were made stronger by the criticism they offered to one another. This collaboration enabled them to advocate for their own learning and to develop skills that they can draw upon in their future teaching lives. As April commented, "This intermediary position as a collaborating advocate—between zero advocacy and individual advocacy—enabled me to embed myself in a safe network of peers while allowing me to practice advocacy strategies that I might eventually have to attempt alone."

Our final example moves to the secondary classroom where April worked during her student teaching experience in a sophomore-level, college-bound English class. This final scenario represents April's move away from her peers into a more isolated position in a secondary classroom.

STUDENT TEACHER ADVOCACY

At the midpoint of my student teaching experience, I was pleased with my students' journaling. While reading Harper Lee's *To Kill a Mockingbird*, they had written on various topics that related the book to their own experiences, all the while using enhanced voice as they told their stories with humor, suspense, and irony. Then, we came to a point in the curriculum where I felt all our progress lurch to a stop: the five-paragraph expository essay.

Because the district writing assessment required students to write an expository essay over the text we had studied, I developed a packet that guided them through the process: topic sentence here, attention-getter there, transitions throughout, and a couple of quotes sprinkled into the mix. I felt as though we were really getting somewhere, until I received a stack of student essays that all sounded the same. Where had my students' vibrant voices gone? When had they become robots in their writing? Why did all of these essays seem to fall in the same place on my scoring rubric? I felt that my student writers had taken a step backward in their confidence and craft in writing. Instead of hearing my students, I heard the boring, monotonous language I had used in the packet. I wondered if they had really learned anything from the process.

Determined to regain my student writers, I launched a creative writing activity with George Ella Lyon's "I Am From" poem. Together we brainstormed ways that the author wrote about her family, capturing the memories that defined where she was from. My students' voices returned as I heard stories that were unique and filled with true emotion. Students revised actively, trying new approaches to their poems. Several Latino students even wrote family sayings in their home languages. This act moved these students, a minority in this school's college-bound classes, to the center of the class. Perhaps, for the first time, these students had found their identity in the curriculum.

When another roadblock arose—an expository essay practice test to help prepare students for the district writing assessment—I spoke with my cooperating teacher. I advocated for a personal narrative approach that would teach the same paragraphing and transition skills as required in an expository essay. I also spoke with other English teachers in the building about my ideas, but all seemed to believe that their hands were bound. As a student teacher with no authority, I was not about to rock the curriculum boat.

My students did take their expository essay test after we discussed how the five-paragraph essay structure can be manipulated for different effects. We used poetry to blend our voices into more formal writing, and most students were able to blend the two forms and arrive at a happy medium in time for the writing assessment. However, I still wonder if this is the best approach for writing. Could my students have achieved better results if they had not been forced to continually practice the essay format? Could other formats and experiences have served the same purpose? Perhaps the most defeating thought is that my hands will be forever tied to issues such as district assessments. I continue to deliberate possible advocacy strategies that I can use to justify more diverse writing approaches.

We include this scenario because we feel that it raises an important issue regarding the different institutional contexts that shape teachers' sense of agency in being advocates. Although April was a leading advocate for changing the curriculum in her pre-service methods course, she still felt limited in her ability to advocate for her students during her student teaching experience. While her pre-service class members offered her a community to draw upon, in her role as student teacher she was viewed as a transitory outsider and as too idealistic to fully understand the realities of classroom teacher. As one teacher told her during her student teaching practicum, "Oh, you're still young. You'll figure it out eventually when you're not quite so energetic." While April sought to engage other teachers in a collaborative effort to develop a more responsive writing curriculum, she found few opportunities for such conversation with her fellow teachers.

Moreover, April felt that she didn't have the authority to advocate against the institutional structure of the district assessment. While in her pre-service methods course she was able to identify a clear audience for her argument, in this context she faced a district mandate—not a "real" person—against which to respond. Indeed, much of her colleagues' reluctance to "rock the curriculum boat" might have been due to a sense of resignation and powerlessness over the role that district assessments played in dictating the curriculum. In short, April continued to feel a gap between what she knew and believed to be true about effective literacy learning practices and her ability to advocate for these practices to colleagues and administrators. Yet this scenario is also hopeful because, despite these experiences, April remains committed to using advocacy strategies in her teaching.

INTEGRATING ADVOCACY WITHIN TEACHER EDUCATION

We have described these scenarios because all represent different forms of and opportunities for advocacy in which teachers engage daily in the English classroom. In conceptualizing teacher education, we believe it is vital to provide opportunities for teachers to explore concepts of advocacy and strategies that they can use to advocate for their students' learning. Moreover we believe that equipping teachers with tools for advocacy can better prepare them to help students advocate for their own purposes. As Beck (2005) suggests ". . . the teacher's role is not only to encourage textual and sociopolitical critique but also to raise awareness of what constitutes responsible voice and action for communicating across spheres and in multiple dimensions: intellectual, emotional, and moral" (p. 399). Unless teachers understand how they can be successful advocates in English classrooms, faculty lounges, parent-teacher conferences, and school board meetings, they cannot possibly encourage such awareness and opportunities for critical engagement with their secondary students. In the spirit of promoting a more critical teacher education experience, we offer the following strategies for integrating concepts of advocacy into English/Language Arts methods courses:

1. The first strategy is to invite teachers (and students) to define what advocacy means in their lives. While advocacy is simply defined as the act of pleading for or supporting, advocacy has negative connotations for some, conjuring associations with strident debaters or militant groups. An initial first step, then, is to elicit the multiple definitions of advocacy that teachers and students hold and to begin thinking through what these definitions might mean (in one's teaching or in one's academic or personal life). For instance, in our own brainstorming, we developed the following working list:

   • Not being afraid to make your own definitions/define your own beliefs and then act toward/on them
   • Making mistakes and using those mistakes to support your new beliefs
   • Keeping evidence (like my student essays vs. their personal writing) to prove that something is really being learned/not learned through a particular practice
   • Speaking up, drawing attention to an important issue and directing decision makers toward a solution
   • Working with other people to make a difference
   • Building support for acting on a problem
   • Realizing that it is a process that involves negotiation, persuasion, perseverance, and even compromise

   Having students and teachers share these brainstorms is an important first step in imagining the multiple ways that they might be advocates because it allows for a general survey of current attitudes and can create forums for sharing experiences related to these definitions of advocacy.

2. An advocacy survey or inventory is another valuable way to surface attitudes and experiences with advocacy. For example, Lewis et al.'s (2005) *Educators on the Frontline: Advocacy Strategies for Your Classroom, Your School, and Your Profession* includes an "Education Advocacy Self-Assessment" (pp. 10–14) in which respondents rate how often they have engaged in advocacy activities such as "met with a group of

teachers to discuss a school issue that concerns you" or "encouraged a group of teachers to protest an action taken by their board of education." Such an inventory can easily be adapted to pre-service teachers or high school students to serve multiple purposes. For one, the survey can surface understandings of advocacy that can be built upon through further exploration. Second, it can provide concrete examples of advocacy that respondents might not have ever considered as "counting" as advocacy work.

3. A third strategy for understanding advocacy is to write an "Advocacy History" where teachers or students examine their prior experiences with advocacy and, based on these experiences, identify advocacy strategies and processes that they've used (either successfully or unsuccessfully) or that they have witnessed others using, and how they have felt about the use of such strategies. Some key questions for such a history might include the following:

   • What are your experiences with advocacy?
   • When have you had to advocate for a particular position/perspective that others discredited or discounted. When have you had to go against the grain?
   • What strategies /processes did you use to make your perspective heard/brought to the table? Did these strategies work? Why or why not? Were the consequences positive or negative? Who controlled those consequences? What was learned? Is there a way that you could have advocated differently with better results?

4. Another strategy for engaging students and teachers in discussions of advocacy is to use case studies related to the types of scenarios in which they might find themselves having to advocate. For instance, Amy developed a case study for her pre-service reading course that borrowed details from a local censorship case. She developed a school board meeting and assigned students various roles (such as parents, a pastor, students, teachers, colleagues, principal) to help them imagine the diverse stakeholders involved in the secondary English curriculum. Such a scenario allowed students to actively engage in controversial issues and to advocate for their "assigned" perspectives in a public, albeit low-stakes, environment.

5. Another activity is to engage students in a brainstorm or clustering of advocacy networks or communities to which they might belong or connect to. As our scenarios illustrate, teachers often feel more empowered to advocate when they are connected to a community or network of like-minded colleagues. Professional organizations, such as NCTE or IRA, are also useful to introduce to students as advocacy resources. For instance, the banned books archive provides teachers

with powerful resources and rationales for teaching controversial texts. Students can see how national teaching communities provide resources on common concerns and issues that teachers face. Teachers also can draw upon advocacy strategies and models outlined in books such as Cathy Fleischer's (2000) *Teachers Organizing for Change: Making Literacy Learning Everybody's Business.*

6. Interviewing teachers or community members who have been identified as exemplary advocates is another way to help teachers and students understand the power of advocacy work. For instance, one local teacher recently redesigned her British literature course to focus on place-based education. Finding out the process she went through to make this curricular shift, and identifying the various issues she faced in doing so, would be highly valuable for teachers to study. Teachers who feel overwhelmed or powerless against institutional or administrative mandates can draw inspiration and concrete strategies from these stories as well as develop networks with fellow teachers.

Overall, we believe that advocacy, as both a concept and tool for action, is central for teacher education. If we are to prepare future teachers for the highly political roles that they inhabit in and outside of the classroom, we must fill the gap in current teacher education programs by providing pre-service candidates with the necessary tools to assert their professional voices in these contexts. Integrating strategies for advocacy awareness into existing pre-service teacher education structures means going beyond the traditional teacher education toolbox of theory and methods to help teachers powerfully advocate for best practices in English education.

REFERENCES

Beck, A. S. (2005). A place for critical literacy. *Journal of Adolescent and Adult Literacy, 48*(5), 392–400.

Danielewicz, J. (2001). *Teaching selves: Identity, pedagogy, and teacher education.* Albany: State University of New York Press.

Fleischer, C. (2000). *Teachers organizing for change: Making literacy everybody's business.* Urbana, IL: NCTE.

Kelly, U. A. (2004). Passionate contracts: Discursive contradiction and struggle in secondary English teacher education programs. In B. R.C. Barrell, R. F. Hammett, J. S. Mayher, & G. M. Pradl (Eds.), *Teaching English today* (pp. 57–67). New York: Teachers College Press.

Lewis, J.J., K. Stumpf, & A. Berger (2005). *Educators on the frontline: Advocacy strategies for your classroom, your school, and your profession.* Newark, DE: International Reading Association.

Ritchie, J. S., & Wilson, D.E. (2000). *Teacher narrative as critical inquiry.* New York: Teachers College Press.

Stenberg, S., & Lee, A. (2002). Developing pedagogies: Learning the teaching of English. *College English 64,* 326–347.

CHAPTER 4

PLACES OF POSSIBILITY, SITES OF ACTION

Reseeing the Gaps between High School and College Writing Instruction

Hephzibah Roskelly and Kathleen J. Ryan

ABSTRACT

We re-envision gaps student teachers experience between their teacher prep-aration courses and field experiences as opportunities for real critical engagement in their work rather than merely regrettable divisions. We find Wolfgang Iser's definition of "gaps" in the reading process provides a useful analogy for considering how gaps between teacher education and teaching in schools might become dynamic sites of interpretive possibility. Paulo Freire's concept of mediation offers a way for teachers to position themselves as active participants who turn gaps into problems to solve, bridges between what is and what could be.

We know gaps loom large on the horizon where teacher education in col-lege meets the high school classroom. Different spaces presuppose gaps, and the classroom teacher seems to be in a vastly different space from the college professor. Both of us now teach in large state universities where we direct writing programs, teach pedagogy courses, and juggle teaching and administration with research and writing. But we both began our teaching careers in the high school. We taught four or five classes a day, coached sports and drama, and juggled those responsibilities with planning, assessing, and mentoring. The demands placed on us as teachers feel equally as heavy in college and high school, but the spaces themselves seem quite separate, the gaps quite real.

Teacher education is rightly invested in closing or bridging some of the gaps that our different spaces create, making the path from one space to another easier to negotiate for the students who will become teachers in a space different from our own. There is much that teacher education can do and is doing to work on that path: listening to those who have walked it, walking it more ourselves, inviting those who've arrived to return to talk about the journey they've taken from university to high school life. Books like Ruth Vinz's (1996) *Composing a Teaching Life* or Curt Dudley-Marling's (1997) *Living With Uncertainty* help bridge divides between teaching in high school and college. On the local level, Kate recently attended a Campus Conference on Teacher Education on the quality of teacher preparation at her university, with participants from teacher preparation programs and from the public schools. Hepsie regularly works with high school teachers across the country teaching Advanced Placement courses, discussing the varying demands of college and high school writing. The potential for bridging gaps between high school and college increases when teachers from these different spaces come together and talk.

When teacher educators engage in mutual dialogue with their high school counterparts and read with their students stories of teachers learning their craft, they alleviate some of the tension that attends the sudden culture shift that student teachers feel once they begin to work in the high school setting. They help build bridges between the two worlds of high school and college by increasing candidates' knowledge and thus developing their skill in meeting the pedagogical demands of the setting they are preparing to enter.

But in this essay we want to look through an alternative lens at the culture shift student teachers experience, not by suggesting ways to close the wide gaps they encounter between one space and another, but by reseeing those gaps as invitations, spaces where student teachers might remake theory and practice for themselves. To help us envision gaps in this way, we turn to reading theorist Wolfgang Iser, whose definition of "gaps" in the interpretive process suggests the inevitability, as well as the necessity, of gaps for making meaning from texts. Students are engaged in reading the world of high school and college as they learn to be teachers, and Iser's ideas about the reading process provide a useful analogy for considering how the gaps between teacher education and teaching in schools might become more the dynamic sites of interpretive possibility than merely regrettable divisions.

In order to learn how gaps are perceived by students and teachers in teacher education and high school, we first describe the results of interviews with several high school teachers and current or former pre-service teachers who comment on the gaps they perceived as they moved from teacher education classrooms to high school classrooms, and on the actions they took to mitigate the gaps they found. We then explore Iser's concept of gaps and of the interpretive process itself in reading, suggesting the connections between his theory and the process teachers must go through in teacher preparation programs and in student teaching. Using candidate interviews and Iser's concepts, we then discuss how to help candidates perceive the gaps they inevitably encounter as opportunities for real critical engagement in their work. An awareness of the usefulness— indeed the need for—gaps in teacher preparation programs, we argue, can stimulate a new means and motivation for expanding the dimensions of teaching literacy in both high school and college classrooms.

WHERE ARE THE GAPS?

Candidates and teachers are deeply conscious of the changes they must go through as they move from the realities of university life to those of the high school. For most of the candidates and teachers we talked with, it was not a smooth or easy transition, and for some, the gap between what they expected to have happen in teaching and what actually did happen remains a painful memory or a current source of frustration.

Hepsie teaches composition pedagogy to undergraduate and graduate English majors and to graduate teaching assistants. Her interviews were with three white males, two experienced high school teachers who took English courses but began high school teaching under North Carolina's lateral entry program, which certifies teachers without education courses or student teaching. The third candidate is in a certification program at the Master's level and is student teaching in the spring.

Kate teaches composition pedagogy to graduate teaching assistants, undergraduate candidates enrolled in West Virginia University's five-year education program, and graduate students enrolled in the teacher certification program. Kate interviewed four teachers, two white women and two white men. One of the men completed his teaching certification in December; he finished student teaching in the fall and has since returned to teach first year composition as an adjunct. The other is student teaching in the spring following a semester teaching first year composition as a GTA.

One of the women is a GTA earning her Master's in English; she student taught as part of her bachelor's in English Education. The other woman is an undergraduate candidate and pre-service teacher enrolled in the five-year program.

Straddling the high school teaching and college teaching spaces, our informants clearly understood the gaps we asked them to describe between high school and college contexts as they responded to these questions:

- What gaps do you see between instruction at the college level and teaching at the high school level?
- How did you see gaps manifested in high school settings?
- How could you or did you fill in gaps you found?
- What might teacher education do to fill in those gaps? What might high schools do to fill in those gaps?
- Are gaps bad?

Our informants spoke at length about the gaps they see in instruction, including concerns with student discipline, teaching grammar and literature, and assigning and evaluating writing. They also worry about the rules and regulations facing public school teachers and the felt pressures of time and the need for dedication and hard work.

Gaps are a source of anxiety for Dawn and Sonya, disrupting their expectations for a seamless transition between college and high school classrooms. Both Dawn and Sonya's high school students are predominantly white and rural, and often have families who struggle economically. Despite the differences in their teacher education programs and their different educational profiles, Dawn and Sonya identify similar gaps in instructional methods, definitions of composition terms, and technology access.

Dawn identifies the way students compose essays in high schools versus college as "the biggest gap I've found." While high school students learn rules for writing a five paragraph essay, where an idea never has more than three parts, college students learn that composing essays is a process of making rhetorical decisions. She describes teaching high school students the "hamburger method," where "you make your top bun and then you fill it with all kinds of stuff and then you slap the bottom on there." Students compose in a "piece by piece approach": "They feel like every paragraph has to start with a topic sentence, and the topic sentence has to state exactly what you're going to do in the paragraph, and they think it has to be five sentences." This five paragraph essay and sequential process are in direct tension with the way she now teaches first year composition, where she teaches students that being a good writer means learning to "apply the different skills you have learned to the situation and the text you are completing." Dawn wishes she could bring this rhetorical approach to high school teaching, and indicates that if she could "go back and change anything, I would want to emphasize to my students that writing is a process, but it is not a process set in stone." However, despite her desire for change, Dawn acknowledges how conflicted she'd feel teaching this way. The "hamburger method" is what she feels she's "supposed to" teach to prepare students for standardized testing in high school, even though it creates confusion for college writers who have to unlearn one way of writing and replace it with another.

Sonya's primary concern is more fundamental than the ones Dawn discusses; she expresses concern simply with getting students to write. Sonya narrates an experience she had when she assigned ninth grade honors students to write an alternate ending to "The Interlopers." To her consternation, only four of the students completed the assignment. Sonya speculates that students might not have done the work because the assignment was unfamiliar. Sonya's host teacher favors repetition of writing assignments linked to readings, while Sonya has been taught to use a variety of activities, including creative and personal writing. The values taught in her teacher education courses—creativity, open-ended assignments, and a student-centered classroom, collided with the host teacher's preference for direct and repeated assignments.

This perceived tension between rigidity and openness also emerges for Dawn and Sonya in considering grammar instruction and evaluation practices. Both feel that high school teachers equate good writing with grammar and define revision as correction, while college professors qualify "good" writing as a situational concern, encourage the teaching of grammar in context, and privilege making meaning over correctness. Sonya, a self-described "grammar queen," definitively identifies high school as "more grammar based," where "you got graded based on red marks," and raises concerns about the lack of a grammar course in her teacher preparation program. Dawn talks about teaching grammar and punctuation in terms of testing: "we were taught to teach to prepare for standardized tests. . . . You're very much taught that your students must know sentence structure, your students must know grammar, they must know comma placement."

Because of testing and the felt need to "teach to the test" (whether national, state, or military), the focus on correction appears to be a nonnegotiable part of teaching high school writing. Dawn says that "[a] lot of times I don't even think public school teachers could tell you why they are teaching what they are teaching, aside from 'there's going to be a test at the end of the year that my students have to pass.'"

Dawn and Sonya also raised technology access as another significant gap. First year writing students at WVU are required to word process writing assignments and use their internet accounts regularly as part of their class work. College teachers can expect students to use the computer facilities on campus if candidates don't have their own computers or printers. Students enrolled in the English Education program at WVU have a series of technology goals to meet to prepare them to work with their future students; however, they quickly learn that socioeconomic inequities in West Virginia mean that many students have little access to computers at home or at school. Dawn's host teacher taught her that "if you were going to require something be typed you give them computer lab time in school because very few of them had computers." Sonya pointed out that students don't learn a process of writing that includes word processing technology, while Dawn discussed that because students handwrite everything, expectations for revision become limited to punctuation and spelling and word changes, while teachers limit the amount of writing to avoid collecting piles of loose and messy drafts.

All these gaps worry Dawn and Sonya; they feel caught between their host teachers and teacher preparation programs, between preparation for standardized testing and expectations for college writing, between what they're learning about teaching writing and what they're "supposed to" teach. For them, gaps are holes in their preparation, large distances they do not feel prepared to cross between the worlds of high school and college writing.

Both Matt and Bill are experienced high school teachers who work in large high schools in North Carolina, one predominantly white and rural and one diverse and urban. Both teach high school Advanced Placement courses as well as a regular curriculum in their departments, and they both entered teaching by routes other than traditional teacher certification programs. As a result, Matt says, "I arrived in the profession top-heavy as far as the academic side of the job was concerned, and absolutely 'green' on the teaching side." Although Matt sees this gap a hole in his preparation, Bill finds that his emphasis on writing in his B.A. program and in later Master's work worked to his advantage: "I don't think I had the 'gaps' that most teachers have."

Still, their concerns about professional training echo many of Sonya and Dawn's concerns. Bill worries that teachers arrive without sufficient preparation for the demands of teaching writing. "What I have observed is that even most English teachers do not know really how to go about teaching writing," he says. He concludes that "it [writing] doesn't seem to be a priority in English education departments." Although Bill cites time as a pressure for all teachers, he worries that new teachers are not taught how *much* time it takes to work with students on rewriting sentences and paragraphs and the entire essay. "I don't mean simply correcting fragments and run ons, but also teaching them how to compose more focused and purposeful sentences with a variety of structures." Bill sees the focus on the "end product" rather than the time-consuming process of teaching writing as a problem for teachers and one not sufficiently addressed in teacher education programs.

For John, a student teacher at a racially and ethnically mixed high school, grammar is a continuing concern and a gap in his college preparation. "I don't have a problem teaching grammar," John notes, "but I know a lot of the other student teachers are finding it difficult." He places the blame on their own instruction at the college level: "Most of their troubles stem from not knowing how to place a comma themselves. I would like to see 321 [English course: Linguistics for Teachers] actually teach grammar." Like Bill, John realizes that grammar needs to be taught in the context of writing, but the focus on "end product" writing in high school writing privileges grammatical correctness, which can be evaluated in right or wrong terms.

Matt and John mention discipline or classroom management issues as big gaps between their expectations of high school teaching and what occurred when they began their work. As John says, "I was completely unprepared for the disrespect that surfaced my first few days." He notes that his problems have lessened, but he's not sure what he did to make improvements. "After the first week or so passed, my discipline problems cleared up, but I don't know why or how. I must've done something right, but I don't know what that something was." Matt suggests that his "greenness" meant that he had to depend on his colleagues to help him understand classroom dynamics and management. "I don't think the breadth of the job is considered. Can it be? Perhaps teachers should be trained more thoroughly in human behaviorism. That should include differences in learning styles for individuals as well as cultural groups and genders."

As is obvious from their comments, gaps are a source of frustration for experienced and new teachers alike. For the student teachers, it is often manifested in their own sense of a lack of knowledge or preparation for a job that seems far larger than they had imagined. For the experienced teachers, there is a sense that much of the job cannot be taught at all but must be learned on site, while the new teachers did not trust high school teachers' practices of teaching writing. Both Matt and Bill noted that the gaps they see might not be able to be filled by instruction at the college level.

For all these teachers though, gaps are figured negatively as a lack or a blank space in a teacher's education, and most saw the fault lying within the college instruction. None suggested that the high school might change its instruction in response. They express the view that colleges have not met the real, practical needs of classroom teachers who teach writing, despite what research teaches about writing pedagogy, or that real knowledge of classroom teaching cannot be taught, making gaps appear unbridgeable. Universities and high schools appear to these teachers to adhere to the ivory tower versus real world stereotype—separated, unequal, and unsusceptible to change.

RESEEING GAPS

Student teachers, as well as faculty in high school and college settings who help prepare those candidates for a teaching life, necessarily engage in interpretive processes: proposing ideas, applying theories, assuming practices. They are, in Wolfgang Iser's terms, both creating and filling *gaps*, and an understanding of how this interpretive process operates for readers suggests strategies for working in the gaps in teacher education.

Iser's (1978) *The Act of Reading* is an exploration of how readers are able to interpret literary work. Iser focuses on the reader, who must bring the text into being in the moment of reading itself: "for that is when the text begins to unfold its potential; it is in the reader that the text comes to life..." (p. 19). As Iser describes it, the text has two poles, one the *artistic*, the author's text, and the other, the *aesthetic*, the reader's evocation of the text (Figure 4.1). Meaning, understanding, interpretation, exist somewhere between the two poles, as the reader makes the text come alive through predicting, challenging, associating, and rethinking in the process of reading. To understand, then, what happens in reading one must concentrate on the interaction between reader and text rather than on authorial technique or on reader's psychology. In other words, making meaning is neither private nor imposed: it is in the *act* of having to move from pole to pole that meaning happens.

Interpretation

A reader is able to make predictions and revise them, to work toward interpretation in a recursive and experiential process, in part because the text itself leaves spaces, gaps, that the reader is invited to fill. No text wants to say everything. Nor can it. In the movement between chapters, the summary sentence like "The next two years passed in a blur," or the setting for a dialogue—and in innumerable other ways—the text does and must leave spaces where the unsaid is spoken by the reader rather than the writer of the text.

Artistic pole   **Aesthetic pole**

(writer's text)   (reader's process)

Figure 4.1.   Iser's notion of poles.

The key point in this description is that gaps are not simply the inevitable result of lack of space or time to write every moment in the fictional world. They are *necessary* for interpretation to work at all. The place for the reader lies in the gaps; a reader finds herself as an active participant in the text as she is constrained to make meaning by projecting her own ideas and experiences into the gaps the text has invited her to fill. As Iser says, "Gaps function as an inducement to communication" (Iser, 1978, p. 35).

How do readers make sense of the gaps or fill them in? Not exclusively with reference to personal experience, Iser tells us. And not by using some predefined set of guidelines alone. Interpretation is experiential and personal: "I've been to San Francisco before, so I understand the setting of the *Maltese Falcon.*" It is likewise governed by situations and conventions: "It's a new chapter," a reader says to himself unconsciously, "There's probably some kind of change in store." Readers use both poles, in other words, to make sense of the blank spaces they encounter in interpreting texts. As they move between these poles, they get better and better at predicting what might happen next, and more and more confident in their ability to make sense of their process and the meaning they are more and more conscious of helping to make.

Seen in this way, gaps are both crucial and positive. They not only promote but demand the kind of critical thinking that teachers are always hoping for from their students. Teachers in training are inescapably caught between the two poles of college and high school classrooms, and they move from pole to pole as they travel to a field site and come back to reflect on it in a teacher preparation class. The space between the two appears very wide to many candidates. As a student teacher said to one of us recently, "It's just two different worlds!" The statement expresses a frightened awareness that the two worlds might be far too different, too far apart to travel between.

What Iser's work suggests, however, puts the candidate at the center of the solution to the problem of filling in gaps and building the bridges that can make travel between the two worlds easier. Those of us who work in English education need to resee the gap as not primarily between high school and college, but between educational structures and candidates learning to be teachers. High school and college together represent one pole, the author's, and they both present situations, beliefs, characters, and conflicts that an observer or a participant in the culture must learn to read. At the other pole is the *reader*, the student teacher who must make sense of the texts presented by the college and the high school (Figure 4.2).

Figure 4.2.   Mapping Iser's notion of poles onto the educational structures student teachers must negotiate.

Interpretation

In a teacher preparation course recently, candidates were asked to consider the theory behind the use of standardized testing in high school English classes. "Is there a theory?" one candidate asked. "I thought it was just that there needed to be some way to show that somebody has learned something." "And how are we supposed to prepare students for them when we never use standard tests in our courses in education or in English?" another asked. As they talked, candidates began to uncover some of the assumptions that guide decisions about evaluation and testing in both college and high school, the varying demands on teachers and on students in each setting. Looking at a sample end-of-course test for eleventh grade and at a final exam for an instructor's literature survey course, they began to speculate about the assumptions that guided the test questions and to consider how their teaching activities might promote both critical thinking for their students and success on exams.

These candidates didn't arrive at final solutions to the considerable problems presented by the high stakes testing required by many school systems nor about the value of essay exams in the college. But what they accomplished was crucial to their development as teachers. They made themselves the agents in understanding and negotiating the gap between how college and high school understand and perform evaluation rather than passive receivers of contradictory beliefs promoted by two different cultures. Becoming problem posers, as writing theorist Ann Berthoff (1982) would say, they began the process of filling in the gaps for themselves.

STUDENT TEACHERS MEDIATING GAPS

As the example from the teacher education classroom above indicates, candidates can locate gaps between the educational structures they are a part of and seek to enter and themselves as interpreters of those structures. For many candidates, however, making this move—reseeing the gap in terms that make them active meaning makers and not passive receivers of conflicting data—comes with difficulty.

The candidate who lamented the "two different worlds" of high school and college saw her work as schizophrenic: she had to make herself into two people, the teacher who spoke the language of high school and the candidate who spoke the completely different language of teacher education in college. She suspected that she didn't understand either language very well, but she was certain that her teacher education course understood the second language not at all. And she was certain that her high school classroom rejected the language—the codes, the theories, the methods—that her college work had taught her to value.

Unfortunately, too many student teachers believe that they are helplessly suspended between the college and high school world, and that belief is understandable when far too many of their teachers at both levels reinforce, directly and implicitly, the gulf between them. High school teachers speak to their student teachers about the "ivory tower" where college professors live far away from the demands of the "real world" of high school. "My cooperating teacher says group work just can't work with these kids. She said you guys just don't understand," the candidate announced. College teachers, perhaps especially English teachers, deny what students have been taught in high school. No three part thesis statement. No prescribed form for formal papers. No research paper. No proscription on the use of first person. "Why do high school teachers have this thing about *I?*" a professor says to her class of student teachers. The new rules that replace the old often seem to candidates just as arbitrary as the ones they are told to abandon: Have a voice. Use details. Show don't tell. Find a form. Use *I*.

Much of their learning throughout their student lives, in fact, has taught candidates to follow rules, whatever they are. Student teachers' experience as learners throughout their educations confirms for them that not only are there unbridgeable gaps between high school and college, but that they are powerless to traverse them. How much of their learning in either setting has centered on inquiry or on posing problems? How much has been truly collaborative? Testing in the high school, coverage in the university, formal constraints that seem to have little to do with the learner as meaning maker, all have made many candidates feel both passive and not responsible for resolving contradiction or ambiguity or unable to imagine possibilities. It's little wonder that student teachers have a hard time seeing themselves as agents who must remake instruction from teacher education courses to meet the demands and contexts of their high school classrooms.

But new teachers can unlearn the lessons that have helped to create their dilemma as they move into their teaching careers. Paulo Freire's work argues that belief is fostered, and changed, with a willingness to act and an assurance that reflection on action will lead to better, and ultimately more hopeful, acts. Freire calls this kind of action "untested feasibility," a metaphor he first uses in *Pedagogy of the Oppressed* (p. 92) to describe what is beyond the "limit situations" imposed by situation or structure. In *A Pedagogy for Liberation*, Shor and Freire (1986) define untested feasibility as the "future we have yet to create by transforming today, the present reality. It is something not yet here but a potential, something beyond the 'limit-situation' we face now, which must be created by us beyond the limits we discover" (p. 153).

How to bridge the divide between student teachers and the structures they encounter in the high school and the teacher education, the "limit situations" of translation of theory to practice, practice to practice in both settings? How to bridge the gaps Sonya, Dawn, and others name? Freire would have learners rely on mediation, a method that brings into relationship the many divisions and gaps candidates encounter. Mediation is no softening of positions, or compromise of ideology; it is instead an action that brings together disparate ideas by considering what is and what might be. It insists that learners themselves bridge gaps, perceive themselves as active, engaged participants who pull together ideas and remake them as they work and reflect. As teachers take on the role of active participants, static institutionalized structures and rules become problems to solve, bridges between what is and what could be.

Matt, the teacher who entered the profession through a "lateral entry" program that allows candidates without training in educational methods to teach, found a large gap between his knowledge of content and his ignorance of method. His first belief was that "I could simply win over students with passion (like something out of a movie.)" He quickly learned that his students didn't necessarily respond to that passion for his subject; they are, he says, "raised to expect an education."

Matt learned to act on the "limit situations" he encountered—apathy, discipline problems, watered down textbooks—through continual practice, through reflecting on that practice, and through talking to other teachers. "I've learned a lot about classroom management with the help of colleagues and with experience." He still feels passion for literature and writing, but now he sees that he can only work toward stimulating that passion in his students with a clear sense of the *how*: the methods he has learned to choose to foster order, responsibility, and respect in his classroom. Some of those methods include a classroom reading journal written and responded to by students, formal presentations by individual students and evaluated by the class, clear guidelines about classroom discussion and turn taking, and group designed in-class writing assignments. The fact that he has come to understand that his teaching revolves more around the students than the subject has allowed him to mediate and to remake the gaps he's found between what he expected and what he encountered. He mediated that gap by locating in his situation what might be as well as what was; he began to see himself not trapped in the gap but a composer of meaning, who could understand the perimeters of the gap and remake them in his teaching.

Marc, who is teaching at a university while seeking a high school teaching job, is anticipating "limit situations" he has learned about as a student teacher and adjunct instructor and will encounter when he has "his own high school classroom"—Standards of Learning, standardized testing, time to respond to student writing, rules with no logic. As a student teacher, Marc felt "bound" by his host teachers' practices, and as a candidate he felt restricted by a teacher's narrowly defined assignments. He describes how he learned as a graduate student to struggle *for* rather than *with* freedom because he had faith in his creativity, he believed in his contributions. When he has "his own classroom" he believes he can mediate curricular requirements with his own ideas about teaching reading and writing. He talks about the risks he's willing to take, the "tricks" he'll employ to "manipulate" limit situations. Marc describes how his host teacher wanted him to focus simply on learning vocabulary when students were reading *The Call of the Wild*, a book students had to read in class since there were not enough books for all the students. Instead of having students read silently at their desks and take vocabulary quizzes as expected of him, he designed a longer unit where the class read the book aloud, pausing to talk about language in context and discuss issues the text raised about nature and survival. In this way Marc both accommodated his host teacher's desire that he teach vocabulary and his insistence that students encounter language in context and engage in the experience of reading the text as a means of talking about significant themes that captured students' interest and imagination. In ways like this, Marc imagines and invents his teacherly self as a problem solver. We believe Marc, like Matt, will continue to mediate gaps because he positions himself as someone with the agency and authority to contend with them.

CREATING OPPORTUNITIES TO COMPOSE GAPS

Teacher educators need to help student teachers turn the gaps between the high school classroom and their college preparation into possibilities, opportunities to compose a teaching praxis. Recognition of gaps as limit situations rather than barriers is an important start toward developing an understanding of teaching as a problem posing activity always located in particular, and contested, contexts.

Just as writers do when they leave spaces for their readers to enter the interpretive process, teacher education classes can create structured gaps for candidates to enter, making gaps in instruction conscious sites for discussion and exploration, and helping student teachers learn to find strategies for exercising their own creativity in altering the limit situations they face.

One way of structuring gaps for candidates is to pose questions about the guiding assumptions and the language we employ in both high school and college settings. Why, for example, is the high school instructor the "classroom teacher" while the college teacher is not? Why are candidates in the "field" only when they're in the high school classroom and not when they're in our own? Why is only one space regarded as the "real world"? The terms employed in these questions illuminate the beliefs we carry, sometimes unconsciously, about the value of the practical, about power and control, and inevitably about the role of the college courses that prepare candidates to teach in the high school classroom.

The topic of teaching composition and technology is one site where we can and should problematize these beliefs. "Technology" is a key word on many college campuses; teacher education programs have technology goals graduates must attain to be "viable" job candidates; faculty are encouraged, if not required, to design class plans integrating technology. Technology has a lot of cutting edge cache in the academy; in secondary education, technology is about access.

The technology gap Kate's informants talk about offers a good example. The technology goals on her campus enumerate a number of abilities—from software use and database and web page construction to communication—candidates must demonstrate to be "good" teachers, but limited student access to technology in the high school prevents teachers from using those skills. In her writing pedagogy course, Kate has offered practice with technology to meet the goals. But after learning from her candidates, she intends to study this gap together with them, asking questions, like "What beliefs inform the teacher education program's technology goals?", "How can teachers adapt technology lessons from college classrooms into high school classrooms when student access is an issue?", and "What professional and pedagogical interests in technology do high school teachers and college teachers have in common and in conflict?" Asking candidates to consider how the kind of activities they do in college using computer technology (from responding to readings in threaded discussions to conducting online research) and how they would adapt these kinds of activities into different high school teaching contexts could give them a way to envision the gaps they'll need to cross in their student teaching. To formalize this inquiry, candidates can turn their own college classrooms and programs into sites to study alongside the high school classes they also observe. Conducting research makes candidates and teachers co-investigators into the gap they observe and co-creators of responses to it, understanding the limit situation and acting to alter it.

The problem that worries our experienced and new teachers most is the teaching of grammar, and like *technology*, the word *grammar* carries a host of different meanings that complicate the ways teachers approach it. Investigating the assumptions that underlie the word gives candidates a structured opportunity to study the grammar gap. Posing questions like, "Why is so much importance placed on grammar in high school and so little in teacher preparation programs?" and "What does it mean to teach grammar in writing courses?", student teachers begin to expose issues of correctness, assessment, rhetoric, literacy, taste, and the array of social, cultural, and educational assumptions that affect the importance assigned to *grammar*. If we know from linguistics that all students are grammatical; that is, they know unconsciously the structures that make up their language and use them fluently all the time, how might that change the way we teach parts of speech? If we know from experience that students have difficulty using punctuation correctly or varying sentence structure, how might that change the way we create writing assignments? Talking with candidates like Dawn and Sonya about why grammar gets taught in required courses in linguistics and composition pedagogy at WVU instead of a grammar course is another way to enter into this conversation.

As they ask these kinds of questions and confront their own experience with grammar instruction, student teachers learn to name their fears, that they don't know terms and so can't correct grammar problems in student writing, or that they won't be doing their job if they don't locate and correct the error on students' work. In a process of considering their experience, observing classes at high school and college levels, reading and talk, student teachers begin, like good readers, to make sense of the gaps they find in both the teaching of grammar and the meaning of the word itself more quickly and use their interpretations more effectively. They begin to allow those interpretations to guide decisions about how to develop the fluency of the students they teach, to make use of their students' own language experience, and to build on that experience.

Student teachers we've taught have used the wide variety of dialects spoken in the classrooms in assignments that ask students to "translate" literary texts into dialect speech or to retell an oral story in dialect speech and in general dialect speech. Others have used children's literature to make their students aware of the linguistic structures they already know and can employ in their writing and teaching. Students find examples of superlatives in newspapers and television talk, and repunctuate lines to change meanings. In all these ways, our student teachers signal their awareness of students' linguistic fluency, of the need to connect grammatical issues and their presence in the world outside of school, and of the variety of grammatical considerations used appropriately in various dialects.

These illustrations suggest that once student teachers re-envision gaps, they begin to make meaning through reflection and action: asking questions, pursuing dialogues, doing research, envisioning change. Bridging gaps requires understanding that gaps are places where the teacher enters to make meaning. As they enter the gaps they find—in technology, grammar, evaluation, authority, time, and a host of others—new teachers learn to compose and recompose them, turning what seem to be intractable problems into workable limit situations. Finding their own Freirean untested feasibility, candidates and teachers bridge the most important gap in literacy education, observing clearly what is and imagining just as clearly what might be.

REFERENCES

Berthoff, A. (1982). *The making of meaning.* Montclair, NJ: Boynton-Cook.

Dudley-Marling, C. (1997). *Living with uncertainty: The messy reality of classroom practice.* Portsmouth, NH: Boynton-Cook, Heinemann Books.

Freire, P. (1984). *Pedagogy of the oppressed* (M. Bergman Ramos, Trans.). New York: Continuum.

Hinkle, M. Personal Interview. 7 March 2005.

Iser, W. (1978). *The act of reading: A theory of aesthetic response.* Baltimore: Johns Hopkins University Press.

Kohan, M. *Re: My Research Project.* E-mail to co-author. 10 April 2005.

Lettieri, S. Personal Interview. 8 March 2005.

McNees, M. E-mail to a co-author. 8 March 2005.

Shor, I., & Freire, P. (1986). *A pedagogy for liberation.* S. Hadley, MA: Bergin-Garvey.

Sizemore, D. Personal Interview. 8 March 2005.

Smith, B. Personal interview. 10 March 2005.

Vinz, R. (1996). *Composing and teaching life.* Portsmouth, NH: Boynton-Cook, Heinemann Books.

Zimmerman, J. E-mail to co-author. 14 March 2005.

CHAPTER 5

CROSSING BOUNDARIES

English Education, Teaching Writing, and Connections to the "Real World"

Kia Jane Richmond

ABSTRACT

English Educators should consider how a focus on writing can help candidates to connect theory and practice. In this chapter, I demonstrate how bridging the gap between writing theories taught at the university level and practices taking place in the secondary schools can be beneficial to both teacher candidates and English Language Arts teachers in the field.

INTRODUCTION

College students enrolled in English Education programs in the twenty-first century are asked to become highly qualified in three areas: selected subject area(s), general teaching strategies, and educational theory. Most state teacher exams are arranged around these special areas, which are also emphasized in content courses, methods courses, internships or field experiences, and student teaching. Though English Education students (here-

Closing the Gap, pages 59–68
Copyright © 2007 by Information Age Publishing
All rights of reproduction in any form reserved.

after called candidates) often take one course in the teaching of writing and are expected to demonstrate writing competence themselves, it is literature, not the study of writing, which is the emphasis of most teacher preparation programs in English. Thus, when candidates begin their careers as full-time English Language Arts teachers, they often find themselves wanting/needing to know more about writing. Some frequently asked questions include the following:

- How can writing help them create assignments and activities that are based in something other than an objectivist (test-oriented) paradigm?
- How can writing engage multiple intelligence?
- How can writing help them connect their content area to another subject or to the community at large?
- How can writing help students to think critically and to develop empathy for others?

Although many professional development opportunities designed for English Language Arts teachers are aimed at helping them invest in district policies or adopted plans for discipline, very few are focused specifically on writing. In this essay, I discuss the design of two English Education classes which are intended to prepare future teachers to incorporate writing into their classrooms and to help newer teachers in the field who might want additional ideas for lesson plans that include writing. My goal is to encourage others in English Education to consider how a focus on writing can help candidates to connect theory and practice. Additionally, I demonstrate how bridging the gap between writing theories taught at the university level and practices taking place in the secondary schools can be beneficial to both teacher candidates and English Language Arts (ELA) teachers in the field.

Each time I teach courses designed to prepare future teachers of secondary English Language Arts, the expanse of our subject area amazes me. According to the National Council of Teachers of English "Standards for the English Language Arts," ELA is defined as a subject that includes reading, writing, speaking, listening, and viewing. In the program in which I teach, three particular courses housed in the English department are intended to prepare secondary students to teach writing, grammar, and literature. Another course taught in Education is focused on reading. *The Teaching of Writing*, one of the two courses I currently teach, prepares students for writing instruction in a variety of disciplines in grades K–12. The other course, *The Teaching of English*, is focused on other areas within English Language Arts (e.g., literature, film, speech, etc.) and on teaching methods appropriate for secondary schools. Candidates in both classes connect theory and practice throughout the semester. They have recently been asked to create lessons plans for graduates of our program who are now teaching English in various states, to design questions for guest speakers to address, and to participate in constructing writing assignments to teach during in-class demonstrations or field experiences. These activities are designed to help candidates understand how concepts and teaching techniques described in texts by experts such as Jim Burke (2003), Nancie Atwell (1998), and Leila Christenbury (2000) might be applicable to teaching in the "real world" (public and private schools around the United States and beyond).

REACHING IN: EXPERIENCED TEACHERS IN THE ENGLISH EDUCATION CLASSROOM

I begin the *Teaching of Writing* class each semester with a discussion of C.H. Knoblauch's (1988) four philosophies of composition, identified as ontological, objectivist, expressivist, and dialogic (p. 128). Following a discussion of these distinct approaches to teaching writing, candidates reflect on how the philosophies of teachers they have observed during field experiences or in their own educations might intersect with Knoblauch's categories. When guest speakers visit the class, they share their philosophies with candidates. Sometimes this is done overtly; in other instances, their approaches to writing are revealed through sample assignments or assessment tools brought from their classrooms. In their journals for class, candidates are encouraged to make connections between what they have read in course texts and what they have observed in field experiences; furthermore, they are encouraged to speculate and ask questions about guest teachers' epistemological positions and instructional choices (Richmond et al., 2006).

A variety of speakers are invited to visit my teacher preparation classes: recent visitors have included a regional *Newspapers in Education* coordinator, the authors of a new composition textbook, and a former ELA student teacher currently working with a local Title VII program. The most popular visitors seem to be local teachers, those working in what candidates refer to as the "real world." One recent guest, a seasoned K–8 teacher, directed students through a writing exercise she uses in her own elementary classroom. Candidates wrote in response to music and created short narratives, which were later shared in a peer response activity. After this experience, candidates deliberated whether these activities and others discussed were similar to those described by Atwell (1998) for a middle school setting and whether they could be implemented successfully in a high school classroom or not. Thanks to the teacher's willingness to share her resources, candidates noticed that many assignments and evaluation strategies shaped for the elementary level may be easily adapted to the secondary writing classroom as well. Visitors from secondary schools have also shared their lessons and experiences.

One local teacher described how she integrates Atwell's writing and reading workshops into her ELA classroom and how that process prepares students to write for/in a variety of settings. She mentioned specifically their continued success on compulsory writing tests as well as in a cross-curricular project focused on a specific historical event. Another visitor, one who teaches English Language Arts to all grades in a rural secondary school, discussed connecting the teaching of high school writing to Howard Gardner's theory of multiple intelligence. Samples of her students' multi-genre projects in response to specific novels or stories were shared with those in my class. Also, she invited candidates to consider the power of performance by describing how her students share poetry they've written at a series of "coffeehouse" readings. While all our methods candidates do field experiences in secondary classrooms prior to student teaching, many do not get to choose which teachers with whom to visit there. Some candidates have come back from observations in various schools with horror stories of journals being corrected for grammar, of writing being given as punishment, and of lessons on "peer response" that were actually editing sessions. Issues brought up by guest speakers often motivate candidates to begin to question the methodologies and theoretical underpinnings of those teachers they observe in the secondary schools.

Visits by classroom teachers have tapped into the university curriculum and highlighted ways that candidates could apply concepts or theories learned from textbooks to realistic teaching situations. Likewise, visitors have reached into candidates' imaginations and encouraged all kinds of metacognitive processing: candidates reflect, consider, and deliberate; they cogitate, evaluate, and synthesize; they posit, wonder, and question everything. This kind of "[s]tudent introspection," Nancy Joseph (2003) argues, "helps us as educators understand student learning" (p. 111). English Education candidates benefit from glimpses that visitors provide into the "real world," and they identify opportunities to hear from veterans in the field as especially meaningful to their professional growth as future teachers.

REACHING OUT—CREATING LESSONS FOR NEW ENGLISH TEACHERS IN THE FIELD

Not long ago, several of my former candidates who are now secondary ELA teachers across the nation have contacted me to ask for assistance in creating lesson plans integrating writing with specific projects in English. One teacher who works in a suburban high school setting asked for help with a unit based on *Fahrenheit 451*. She explicitly requested that we (my methods class and I) try to incorporate projects that weren't tied to an objectivist paradigm, since she had enough (test) materials from that position. I presented her appeal to candidates in my Teaching of English class, who excitedly separated into two groups and created a series of lesson plans applicable to the novel, with the appropriate state standards and suggestions for assessment. These lessons included a trial for one of the characters and a request for the high school students to construct artistic representations of the novel's setting. We emailed the plans to the teacher and received a positive response along with details as to why she decided to wait to use the lessons the next time she teaches the novel.

Another teacher asked for help in creating lessons that would help her get to know her high school students better as individuals and as members of a culture with which she had little personal experience. Candidates in my class researched Native American art (hoping to learn more about the culture of the students) and developed a five-day lesson plan connecting personal identity to the concept of creating mandalas. Candidates familiarized themselves with the appropriate state standards and delved into making lesson plans, handouts, assessment rubrics, and art project ideas to share with the teacher. After sending our materials, we received a note of thanks from the teacher which stated that though she wasn't sure when she would employ the lessons, she would be able to implement them at some point this year. Later in the term, as we talked about why teachers might ask for ideas and then not use them right away, candidates examined a set of entry-level standards for teachers in our state and discussed their beliefs about (and illusions of) the teaching profession during the first few years. Most began to consider how overwhelming the task of preparing for a set of ELA classes might be in one's own state, let alone in a new geographic (and cultural) area.

It has been only recently that I have realized the benefits to be reaped by candidates who have been asked to connect theories learned in methods courses to practices in the secondary schools. They feel empowered while working on these lessons and gain a sense of purpose and self-confidence as future ELA teachers. Several commented that this activity (creating lesson plans for teachers in the field) is one of the first times they've been able to take strategies learned in Education classes and concepts learned in English classes and put them together. Likewise, the novice teachers noted that being reminded of strategies/theories learned in their own methods courses is useful and that once their memories are triggered, these educators are reenergized. They then tend to make more connections between theory and their own practices or those of neighboring teachers.

Kathy Megyeri (1999), a veteran English teacher in Maryland, observes that it is "new teachers who are dedicated and excellent role models [which] are like candles that light others while consuming themselves"

(p. 24). Candidates and newer teachers need to be rekindled in order to continue illuminating others. By encouraging candidates to reach beyond the university classroom, we help them gain experience constructing lessons— connecting standards and writing theory with instructional methods—and we offer these future teachers glimpses into the "reality" of negotiating theory and practice in their early teaching careers. An additional benefit of having future English teachers create lesson plans that are based on ideas or requests from current teachers in the field is that those teachers represent a picture difficult for many candidates to envision. Working as a full-time teacher in a real secondary ELA classroom is hard to imagine when one is up to one's ears in other people's theories and little of one's own practice.

REFLECTING ON CONNECTIONS BETWEEN THEORY AND PRACTICE

Relating theory and practice seems valuable to both secondary teachers working in the schools and candidates in our university programs. How, then, can we in English Education continue to design effective lessons for our candidates that help them to relate theoretical issues to pragmatic ones? One suggestion is to offer candidates opportunities to formulate and ask complex questions. In a recent discussion of journaling, one of my English Education candidates asked how high school teachers deal with issues of self-disclosure in students' writing. His question did two things: First, it encouraged me to consider existing writings related to self-disclosure, and I recommended that students look at publications by Morgan (1998) and Bardine et al. (2000), among others. Second, the question led me to redirect candidates toward generating related questions and seeking out information from teachers and other stakeholders in the schools where they were doing field experiences (e.g., What do teachers in local schools do when secondary students write about physical or emotional abuse? Who should one talk to first when a student writes poetry focused on suicidal thoughts or self-image problems?).

Unfortunately, candidates do not always take the time to ask the questions they have during class unless persuaded to do so. Therefore, I invite candidates to ask questions at several points during the semester, written in class on index cards; these questions are to be answered during the same period, if possible. Answers are based on research and theories in English Education (in published texts, through Internet sources, and from ideas shared by guest speakers) and on my own experiences as a classroom teacher and teacher educator. The routine of questioning promotes the creation of associations between educational theory and instructional approaches in ways that supplement candidates' responses to assigned readings or questions that might be generated during field experiences.

Here are two examples of questions candidates have asked and answers I have offered. (1) *What can candidates do when a student shares in a journal that she has been cutting?* Talking to the school counselor is a good first course of action. Self-mutilation (defined as self-inflicted violence, whether it is cutting the skin, burning oneself, etc.) is a serious issue. We, as teachers, need to be informed; therefore, I recommend looking into research on the issue before attempting to respond to the student. (2) *How do candidates deal with students who write about depression or suicide, or who choose to research those subjects when given choices during a project?* First, it's not uncommon for adolescents to feel depressed or to be interested in psychological issues. It's important to let students know that writing about being depressed can be one of many ways of dealing with the problem. Sometimes getting feelings out on paper (or computer) helps one feel a sense of release; at other times, counseling or medication is a more effective response. In addition to writing, talking to a counselor, doctor, or helpline can be a way to manage depressive episodes. However, we must make clear that suicide is not an acceptable coping strategy. Referring students who indicate suicidal tendencies is a must, and candidates should feel comfortable asking their cooperating teachers about school policies related to referrals whenever a life is on the line.

It seems that questions about self-disclosure in student writing are becoming commonplace in the English Education classroom or student teacher seminar. Why might that be the case? Dan Morgan writes that "students' topics and concerns, and their life experiences and points of view, reflect what has been occurring in our society at large. Our students write about violence and substance abuse and broken families because they're writing about what they have lived and witnessed firsthand, what they care most deeply about" (p. 325). It's likely that candidates are asking more questions related to self-disclosure because more self-disclosing is happening in the English high school classroom. It's also possible that the number of questions being generated is related to candidates' training in *responding* to students and their writing as opposed to merely *grading* student writing.

Active research is also an activity that can help candidates to use questioning as a means to bridge the gap between what is happening in the schools and what experts and researchers say should occur there. Candidates should take questions they have about educational models or concepts learned during coursework at the university and delve into research in our classes. They need to figure out how teachers make decisions about texts, instructional methods, assessments, and technology; this research invites them to interconnect theory and practice. Often, for instance, they want to find out more about educational practices related to specific issues in the teaching of writing.

For example, one candidate in my *Teaching of Writing* class elected to research the issue of autism and writing. She considered her personal experiences, did textual research to find strategies identified as useful in the teaching of writing for students diagnosed with autism, then drafted the essay, reworked it through multiple peer and teacher responses, and submitted it for publication. Her essay was made available to other English teachers throughout the state (Buehrly, 2005), and has sparked many conversations about teaching writing to students with special needs. Inviting candidates to develop questions into research can help them construct associations between teaching practices and education theories; furthermore, introducing candidates to the idea of research as an integral component of classroom teaching can lead them to seek out opportunities for "educational action research" (actionresearch.altec.org) or "teacher research" (www.exchange.org/multicultural/tar) when they are working in their own English Language Arts classrooms in the schools.

One additional thought is that candidates in English Education programs should engage in the writing process at the university level: they should be encouraged to free write, to write in groups, to experiment with graphic organizers, and to revisit their assignments throughout the semester. Using class time for peer response and editing will confirm to candidates that writing is a valued set of practices and not merely a means to an end (product). Candidates should write multiple drafts, participate in holistic or portfolio assessment as well as in traditional methods of evaluation. In my own *Teaching of Writing* class, I introduce candidates to a variety of ways of responding to and grading writing. In addition to discussing theories from Elbow's (1993) "Ranking, Evaluating, and Liking," candidates also reflect on methods of evaluation that they remember from their own schooling or that they have observed being used in the schools in which they do their field experiences. This practice, in addition to my employing a method of holistic grading (portfolio pedagogy) in my classes, encourages candidates to consider the contradictions or disparities between theories about writing taught in the university and practices of writing and assessment in the secondary schools.

Along with asking candidates to reflect on writing as a process, university teachers of English Education should invite future teachers of writing to attempt to construct non-written projects in order to experiment with fitting Gardner's theory of multiple intelligence into the ELA classroom. Considering connections between writing and music, imagery, logic, and the other intelligences can assist candidates in constructing schemas for writing as only one of many ways of thinking and interacting in the world. Many ELA teachers in the secondary schools work with Gardner's theories, asking their students to create multi-genre projects in response to literature or film. However, at the university, the focus remains on (argumentative, researched) writing. Future teachers should be able to evaluate student work in a variety of formats; therefore, I include both written and non-written assignments in my methods classes. In addition, I ask ELA candidates to pay attention to how thinking is expressed in student work in the secondary schools and to reflect on that work in their journals. It is this kind of cognitive activity (metacognition) that helps candidates relate what they know to what they will teach. What's more, candidates in my classes develop a greater sense of empathy for experienced teachers and those secondary students who are in their classes.

Asking candidates/teachers to make connections between personal experiences, educational theories, and classroom practices should be a strategic focus of any program designed to prepare or support teachers of English Language Arts. Crossing boundaries between theory and practice in the university classroom will require us to create assignments that ask candidates to reflect and think metacognitively and to engage in processes that they will ultimately use in their own classrooms. Additionally, reaching beyond university walls to connect ideas about lesson planning with authentic writing/literature instruction will help English Education candidates better prepare for the challenges of working in a discipline in which one often feels isolated and perhaps limited by resources that are determined by shrinking educational budgets. English Education candidates who have had the chance to work with teachers in the schools (who comment on instructional strategies developed in conjunction with relevant educational theories) should be better able to think critically and to anticipate how their lives will change as they move back and forth in praxis, shifting from theory to practice and back again. Reflecting on ways to improve communication between classroom ELA teachers and those who will work with them as observers, student teacher candidates, or new colleagues can only serve to enhance the relationships that they will build with one other, their middle school or high school students, and their students' writing.

REFERENCES

Atwell, N. (1998). *In the middle: New understandings about writing, reading, and learning*. Portsmouth, NH: Boynton/Cook.

Bardine, B. A., Bardine, M.S., & Deegan, E.F. (2000). Beyond the red pen: Clarifying our role in the response process. *English Journal*, *90*, 94–101.

Buehrly, B. (2005). All children can write! Teaching strategies for helping children with autism. *Language Arts Journal of Michigan*, *21*, 65–67.

Burke, J. (2003). *The English teacher's companion: Complete guide to classroom, curriculum, and the profession* (2nd ed.). Portsmouth, NH: Heinemann.

Christenbury, L. (2000). *Making the journey: Being and becoming a teacher of English/ Language arts.* Portsmouth, NH: Boynton/Cook.

Educational Action Research. ALTEC, University of Kansas. (www.actionresearch.altec.org). Accessed October 31, 2005.

Elbow, P. (1993). Ranking, evaluating, and liking: Sorting out three forms of judgment. *College English, 55,* 187–205.

Gardner, H. (www.howardgardner.com). Accessed November 3, 2005.

Joseph, N. (2003). Metacognition in the classroom: Examining theory and practice. *Pedagogy, 3,* 109–113.

Knoblauch, C.H. (1988). Rhetorical constructions: Dialogue and commitment. *College English, 50,* 125–39.

Megyeri, K. (1999). Insights for interns: To student teach. *English Journal,* 20–25.

Morgan, D. (1998). Ethical issues raised by students' personal writing. *College English, 60,* 318–325.

Richmond, K. J. (2003). Academic service learning in an English methods class: A practical approach. *Language Arts Journal of Michigan, 19,* 8–12.

Richmond, K. J., Baker, D., Brockman, E., & Bush, J. (2006). Composition studies/ English education connections. *The Writing Instructor. MACROBUTTON HtmlResAnchor* www.writinginstructor.com.

Smagorinsky, P, Cook, L. S., & Johnson, T. S. The twisting path of concept development in learning to teach. CELA Research Report Number 16002. (www.cela.albany.edu/publication/abstract/smagorinsky)

Teacher Action Research. Ed Change. (www.edchange.org/multicultural)

CHAPTER 6

THE ROLE OF THE NATIONAL WRITING PROJECT IN CLOSING THE GAP BETWEEN TEACHER PREPARATION AND TEACHING WRITING IN SECONDARY SCHOOLS

Matthew Kilian McCurrie

ABSTRACT

This chapter presents evidence from national assessments, like the National Assessment of Educational Progress (NAEP), about what improves student writing and what represents the most promising strategies and classroom practices. This chapter will demonstrate the ways the National Writing Project has been a key force in not only the professionalization of teachers in the schools, but also in helping teacher candidates connect writing theory and practice. Focusing on examples of partnerships between university instructors and writing project sites, this essay shows how writing project teacher-consultants, university instructors, and teacher candidates can productively collaborate.

Closing the Gap, pages 69–83
Copyright © 2007 by Information Age Publishing

69

IDENTIFYING AND UNDERSTANDING THE GAP

The place of writing in student learning is central, and although the truth of this statement is widely accepted, the strategies, programs, and plans developed to address the importance of writing have only reached a fraction of students. Unfortunately, except for college-level teaching geared to the first-year writer, composition pedagogy remains a neglected area of study at most of the nation's schools of education, where future teachers are trained. Content knowledge and access to the latest research and materials are essential to teacher expertise and reflect directly on student achievement and performance. The 1996 National Commission on Teaching and America's Future cites studies showing that teacher qualifications account for 40% of the difference in overall student performance and that good teaching is a more powerful influence on learning than a student's socioeconomic background.

Findings like these support and energize the National Writing Project and English educators' efforts to improve student literacy through writing. NCTE reports, however, that very few states require specific coursework in the teaching of writing for certification. A survey of state requirements conducted for the NWP publication, *Because Writing Matters: Improving Student Writing in Our Schools* (2003), supports NCTE's data: Missouri, Delaware, and Idaho are the only states that specifically require coursework in the teaching of writing for licensure. While most states now test potential teachers on their basic writing abilities and writing expertise is assumed in many state competency requirements, this too varies widely. Some requirements, like Vermont's, expect knowledge of the composing process as well as the ability to teach writing across the curriculum, but examining coursework and competency requirements, it is clear that writing requirements lack rigor when compared to reading requirements. The importance of the teaching of reading is reflected in both competency standards and required coursework, but writing does not receive this attention. Even though research shows that literacy entails reading and writing and the two are best learned together, teacher preparation does not reflect this.

FILLING THE GAP: THE NATIONAL WRITING PROJECT
AND ITS ROLE IN IMPROVING THE TEACHING OF WRITING

Since 1974 the National Writing Project (NWP) has focused on improving writing and learning in our nation's schools by connecting teachers and creating networks devoted to teachers teaching teachers. A distinctive feature of its approach has been bridging the gap between K–12 and post-secondary teachers. The summer institutes sponsored by affiliates of the

National Writing Project remain one of the few places where teachers, administrators, and university teachers join as peers to develop themselves as writers and writing teachers. Colleges have struggled to define what students need to know and be able to do in order to be successful writers, and teacher preparation programs, a logical place to bring these two things together, have often neglected this need. The local writing project site may be one of the few places where these various disconnects and problems of vagueness can be addressed.

The NWP (2005) reports that its professional network presently links 185 college-based sites in fifty states, Washington, DC, Puerto Rico, and the U.S. Virgin Islands. Annually, the NWP sponsors more than five thousand professional development programs through its sites, including three thousand in-service workshops, more than a third of these are part of an ongoing partnership with a school. One reason for the popularity of these workshops is the fact that they are led by highly skilled and experienced teachers. Two features of the NWP's approach to teacher development seem to set it apart: an awareness of the social and relational practices that motivate and sustain teachers; and small informal networks that organize and extend relationships among the larger, more formal writing project groups. These small communities produce new forms of support, revitalizing the commitment and support for the larger organization. By putting teachers' expertise and local networks at the heart of its professional development model, the NWP has flourished, influencing teachers across traditional boundaries of level and subject.

THE ROLE OF ASSESSMENT IN IMPROVING THE TEACHING OF WRITING

The professional development model developed by the NWP also depends on using the most current research into the teaching of writing. Careful analyses of writing assessments can provide insight into what helps students learn to write. One study of writing achievement levels the NWP has relied on is the 1998 National Assessment of Educational Progress (NAEP) report card on writing, published by the U.S. Department of Education. The NAEP report studied students' performance in grades four, eight, and twelve and found links between performance on the writing assessment and school practices. High achieving students cited specific practices like planning and drafting as important to their success as writers. Students in grades 8 and 12 that were asked to plan their writing at least once a week or more outperformed their peers who were never or hardly ever asked to consider planning what they wrote (Greenwald et al., 1999).

A correlation was also found between high student scores and the practice of writing multiple drafts. Students in grades 8 and 12 that regularly produced multiple drafts of writing assignments had higher average scores than those students who were not required to do so (*NEAP 1998 Writing Report Card for the Nation and the States*). The NAEP report also found that two teacher practices contributed to higher scores: the use of portfolios and engagement in meaningful classroom discussion. The NAEP report reveals "a positive relationship was evident between teachers talking with students about what students were writing and students' writing scores. This was more evident at grades 8 and 12 than at grade 4; at grades 8 and 12, students whose teachers always spoke with them about their writing outperformed their peers whose teachers sometimes spoke with them about their writing" (*NEAP 1998 Writing Report Card for the Nation and the States*). All three grade levels registered the positive influence of portfolios on student scores.

NAEP has also studied the relationship between reading comprehension and writing and found that students benefit the most from curricula that vary and integrate both reading and writing. Students who completed frequent and varied reading and writing assignments demonstrated greater levels of achievement on standardized assessments like NAEP. The NWP has used the NAEP data and conclusions to extend the uses of writing throughout the curriculum, across both level and subject areas. NAEP's 1998 findings reinforce findings from their other comprehensive studies of the teaching of writing. A 1992 NAEP report concluded that "teaching the cluster of writing techniques known collectively as 'writing process' is associated with higher average writing proficiency among students. Students whose teachers always had them do such activities, especially in combination, had the highest average writing scores. Students who did certain pre-writing activities on the actual NAEP test also had higher average proficiency scores than other students" (*NAEPfacts*). NAEP found that the problem-solving skills involved in the process approach gave students a range of strategies for all parts of the process: pre-writing, planning, discovery drafts, as well as giving and using feedback from various sources. The report echoed the meta-research conducted by George Hillocks that found writers who spend less time planning and revising perform the poorest on writing assessments. Hillocks argued that skilled writers "pay attention to content and organization, while weaker writers are more preoccupied with the mechanics of writing, especially spelling. Good writers are found to use a longer pre-writing period than average writers" (Hillocks, 1986, p. 28).

The 2002 NAEP report reveals the effects of increased emphasis on meeting the reading and math benchmarks of No Child Left Behind (NCLB). Only 49% of high school seniors received writing assignments of three pages or more, and then only once or twice a month. Thirty-nine percent reported receiving such assignments "never" or "hardly ever" (National Commission on Writing, 2003, p. 20). These most recent statistics suggest that writing instruction may be even less a priority today than it was prior to NCLB. Although most high school graduates can produce basic, formulaic writing, the study found that few can produce writing that is precise or engaging (NAEP, 2002 cited in NCW, 2003, p. 16).

Research also demonstrates that writing is complicated to teach, and it is often thought of as just a single school subject, learned once and tested. In fact, it is much more than this, and learning to teach writing effectively requires attention to constantly changing contexts and knowledge of students' instructional needs. Writing is not a subject that can be learned in one course, at one time, for a student's entire educational life, even though this is sometimes inferred from large-scale assessments. Without teachers and administrators who value, understand, and practice writing, we cannot build a nation of effective communicators. States like Alaska, Washington, and Montana have identified writing in content areas as a key learning target for students in middle and high school, and all of the national organizations for subjects like math and science have included writing as part of their standards.

Eighteen states now require students to pass a writing test to graduate from high school. Several others including Alaska, Washington, and Idaho—will soon follow. Students planning to attend college also face new writing assessments for college admission. Beginning in 2005, both the SAT and ACT have included a writing section on their exams. No group will be more impacted by these new writing demands than low-income students and nonnative speakers of English who represent a large portion of college students who must take pre-college-level writing courses. Often these courses require additional fees that cannot be paid for with financial aid, and do not count toward graduation, creating major obstacles to college success (Jennings & Hann 2002).

CONNECTING TEACHER CANDIDATES, NEW TEACHERS, AND EXPERIENCED TEACHERS THROUGH THE LOUISIANA STATE UNIVERSITY WRITING PROJECT

The National Writing Project has a long history of working with many groups representing governments, state boards of education, and local school districts to extend and develop the kinds of practices that NAEP and other studies have identified as most effective in the teaching of writing. Local sites of the NWP have been at the forefront of offering the best teachers advanced professional development opportunities through its summer institutes and continuity programs. As the overall educational environment has changed, the NWP has also adapted, maintaining its focus on extending and developing the teaching of writing through a teachers-teaching-teachers model. In the NWP site located at Louisiana State University the directors and board sought ways to adapt to the changing contexts and expectations for the teaching writing. While leadership still wanted to make available opportunities for highly experienced teachers to advance their knowledge and pedagogy, local school districts (called parishes in Louisiana) had an even greater need to meet: the overwhelming number of teachers and teacher candidates that had little teaching experience and in some cases no background in the teaching of writing. Local parishes were using all their professional development resources to improve the basic qualifications of their teachers. For a time it appeared as though writing theory and pedagogy would be marginalized, but the local writing project sites in Louisiana began to react creatively. The LSU Writing Project made a few seemingly small changes, but they made a significant impact on new teachers and teacher candidates.

For years, LSU Writing Project maintained a continuity program through its regular All Project Meetings held at local schools on Saturday mornings. Usually, this was a chance for teachers who had completed the intensive summer writing institute to reconnect with the community of friends and colleagues from the writing project. Most often these meetings would be organized around a theme like "Writing in the Gifted and Talented Classroom" or "Using Technology Effectively in the Writing Workshop Model," and included time for teachers to work in groups, sharing their own writing. Even though these meetings were successful, the effects did not "trickle-down" to less-experienced or under-prepared teachers. This fact made it difficult for local parish school boards to support the writing project, even though it certainly helped some teachers.

When the LSU Writing Project's leadership realized that there were many more teachers who could benefit from these meetings, it was decided to make an effort to invite all teachers, especially new teachers and pre-service teachers. University candidates enrolled in methods courses were also encouraged to be a part of the writing project because their crowded schedules left little room for an extra writing course, and the methods course itself could only provide limited attention to the teaching of writing. For many new teachers, who did not have the time, energy or money to invest in a course at the university during the busy school year, open writing project meetings provided a key source of assistance. By opening monthly meetings to all colleagues and future colleagues, the meetings doubled in size and also gave the most experienced teachers an opportunity to help newer teachers. The amount of time that had often been devoted to speakers was now limited, and showcases of lessons and units were planned to demonstrate how to incorporate LA standards with the best practices that have been developed through research.

These monthly meetings became a way for newer teachers and pre-service teacher candidates to experience the actual lessons that their experienced colleagues developed and used successfully with their students. In one showcase session, university students could see how an experienced teacher responded to student drafts. Participants in this session were given the opportunity to apply these newly acquired strategies to samples of student writing in both early stages of drafting and more polished versions. As useful as a secondary methods class can be, there was really no way to re-create this kind of opportunity for students. Not only were teacher candidates getting experience responding to drafts, but they were also getting to pose questions and see how a group of highly qualified teachers go about troubleshooting the exigencies of the classroom.

At the midterm and end of the semester, teacher candidates enrolled in the methods course completed a survey and reflection. This data reveals the powerful impact made by the writing project meetings. When asked to describe a significant learning experience, many teacher candidates chose to write about one of the writing project meetings they attended. Teacher candidates describing the response session expressed feelings of being overwhelmed when they looked at the piece of writing projected on the overhead. Several teacher candidates also described being distracted by the grammatical errors they immediately noticed in the student draft. While the methods course tried to both model good response for students and provide opportunities for them to respond to each others' writing, being confronted by a 9th grader's first draft was a very different experience for teacher candidates. Several teacher candidates also expressed some frustration at both the midterm and end of the semester since they hoped to find or be given a formula for responding to students' drafts. What they experienced at the writing project meeting on response was not a formula. As experienced teacher consultants volunteered to write a response to the piece projected on the overhead, teacher candidates began to see, not a formula, but a repertoire of strategies:

- Identify possible audiences for the piece and suggest how each audience might require a different path of revision
- Identify possible purposes for the piece and suggest how purpose might require a different path of revision
- Identify possible genre or forms this writing could take (satire, biography, essay, letter to editor, brochure, dramatic dialogue)
- Identify possible areas for further research

Teacher candidates learned that good writing teachers may respond differently to a first draft and still provide useful feedback for the writer.

Monthly meetings also gave experienced teachers an opportunity to share ideas about how to provide students with feedback through conferencing. Teachers briefly explained how they organized these mini-conferences while students were involved in writing workshops, according to Nancie Atwell's description in *In the Middle*. Teacher candidates were already familiar with Atwell's use of mini-conferences, but the experienced teachers provided concrete examples that provided a vivid picture of a best practice. Some teachers shared prompts and worksheets that give the mini-conference focus and meaning.

Conference Worksheet

K. McCurrie

During this week we will use our writing workshop time to get feedback on our Persuasive Essay. You will also have a ten minute conference with me to discuss your draft. Fill out these questions carefully so that we can use our time effectively in the conference. Since part of your grade for this essay will include how well you have drafted and revised, you should be prepared for this conference.

Please fill in the blanks.

So far I have been able to accomplish _____. My topic has developed from _____ to _____. I still have major questions about _____, _____, _____. I'm most happy with these changes that I've made: _____, _____, _____. My responding readers have suggested _____, _____, _____. I followed _____'s suggestions because _____, and I ignored _____'s because _____. In the conference I want to find out about _____.

When teachers share concrete ways they have developed important techniques like responding and conferencing, newer teachers and teacher candidates can begin to build a large reference of strategies and approaches that they would not encounter in one methods course taught by one teacher. Once teachers have an example like the conference worksheet they can then begin to discuss how it could be adapted for many different subjects and levels.

In addition to the discussions concerning response, teacher candidates also valued the all-project meeting devoted to creating opportunities for students to publish what they write. While many of the English methods texts, like Atwell's (1998) *In the Middle*, stress the importance of audience and publication as ways to demonstrate to students how their language functions to communicate, teacher candidates and newer teachers struggle to help students regularly publish their work. The all-project meeting showcase format gave experienced teachers the opportunity to share the many ways their students publish their work. Amy Greenbaum Clark, a writing project consultant, shared two specific examples from her own classes that teacher candidates found helpful.

Mission Impossible: Writing a Class Mission Statement

Amy Greenbaum Clark

This is an excellent first day activity as it gets students setting goals and thinking about writing for an audience immediately.

The mission statement activity can be implemented and/or modified many times throughout the year as the mission of the class/individual changes.

It is vital that students understand exactly what a mission statement is before attempting to write one.

What Is a Mission Statement?

Expresses a goal
Uses a positive and professional tone
Requires concise writing

Who Uses Them?

Major corporations
Small businesses
Government officials and government agencies
Schools
Individuals (athletes, students, etc.)

Why Write One?

It is important to understand and know what goals are set
It is easier to achieve goals if they have been expressed in writing and we have easy reference to them.

After This Explanation

I usually have students brainstorm individually what they feel are the components of a successful class before beginning the activity.

We list the components on the board.

We work from this list to create a mission statement that represents the goals of that individual class.

Typically, there is one student writing the mission statement on the board as the class composes it and one student writing a hard copy at their desk.

The final draft is copied into notebooks and also written decoratively by a volunteer on a piece of poster board.

All class mission statements hang in the classroom for all to see until they are revised.

Small Group Publishing Opportunities

Amy Greenbaum Clark

Teaching background information on *The Crucible*—*The chance for you to show me the way you wish you could be taught.*

My Dilemma!

Notes on the overhead—boring

Lecture notes = daydreaming and sleeping audience

It is time for you to get some background knowledge on *The Crucible*, but there is a lot of information and I do not want to bore you with two days of lectures! So here's the plan:

> You will first sign-up for a topic related to *The Crucible*. Sign-up for one that sounds interesting, as it is more important for you to like your topic than the people in your group.

> There are four spaces under each topic and no more. Once you are situated in your group, you will research your topic and develop a creative and substantive lesson to teach the class.

The Specifics:

Day One: Choose groups, develop a list of 10 questions you wish to answer about your topic, and make a list of different ways you might be able to present your information as a group.

Day Two: Begin your research: take notes, highlight, and outline. I expect you to get a good amount of research done on this day.

Day Three: Finish your research. Then come together as a group and determine which information is important enough to include in your presentation. Turn in an outline for what you will present. LAST DAY FOR RESEARCH.

Day Four: Finalize your lesson plans in the classroom. I will give you a very specific format for the lesson plan.

You will have to give the lesson topic, your objectives, your activities (how you will present the material—handout, overhead, oral notes, interactive activity, video, media) and how you plan to evaluate (ensuring that students understood and retained the information).

Both of the activities Greenbaum Clark shared were helpful to teacher candidates because they demonstrated how abstract concepts like audience or classroom publishing can look. Teacher candidates saw ways to write directions, organize activities and motivate students. In the first handout, Greenbaum Clark addressed teachers directly providing her own commentary on the activity, and in the second handout she showed how she addresses students. Another advantage of Greenbaum Clark's presentation was that the activities she offered were common enough that other teachers could add how they extended or altered these activities. Teacher candidates did not receive just two activities to incorporate into their teaching, but multiple possibilities for each activity Greenbaum Clark presented.

The midterm and end of semester data gathered from teacher candidates in the methods course also showed that they were learning about how the crosshatching of friendships in the writing project created a sense of community. Many teacher candidates described how surprised they were at the overall atmosphere of the writing project meetings. It was obvious that they had many assumptions about how writing teachers behave. Teacher candidates mentioned how they thought they would be stuck in a very formal setting where they would be listening to experts, but found that they felt very comfortable and that others encouraged their participation.

Even newer teachers benefitted from this exchange since many of these teachers were in schools that did not have a teacher that could be a resource on writing issues. The project meetings also gave new teachers a chance to test and revise ideas for their own assignments. For example, one first-year teacher wondered why students couldn't successfully complete even a simple writing assignment like "describe your bedroom using specific details." Her more experienced colleagues suggested she revise her assignment providing more structure and scaffolding for students' ideas. She left that project meeting with a revised assignment: "Describe your bedroom for a classmate who hasn't seen it. Your description should include enough detail so that when a classmate reads it, she or he will be able to tell what you like, what your interests are, and what's important to you." Teachers added that students' descriptions should be posted for classmates to read and identify. Best practices emphasize the importance of framework and guidelines for assignments, but newer teachers do not always have the experiences and mental pictures of the best practices they read about in university classes. These kinds of events are also successful because they help newer teachers with the immediate concerns of their classrooms as well as increasing their repertoire of what best practices look like.

Regular monthly meetings also provided teacher candidates and new teachers an opportunity to write. Writing teachers must write. This expectation derives from the deep conviction of NWP that in-service in the teaching of writing must be grounded in the practice of writing. Participants in monthly meetings are drafting and revising in the same ways that the NWP advocates students should. One of the aspects of the monthly meetings that teachers reported as most transformative was the time for writing and revising. Many teacher candidates and new teachers have not had the experience in college courses of doing multiple drafts, reading their drafts aloud, or getting feedback that is not exclusively focused on grammar and syntax. Once they realized the importance of using multiple drafts and feedback, they sought ways to incorporate some of these practices into their own classes. For example, a new biology teacher who worried about spending time on writing instead of covering content worked with a writing project consultant to look at different ways to incorporate these writing principles in a high school science class. Since modern biology instruction requires hands-on inquiry, not just lab reports, the biology teacher adopted a pre-lab approach that he called his "think-through-the-problem approach."

After using drafting and revising himself, this teacher concluded that writing could be a means for students to think through and think about a problem. Through writing that allowed students to speculate and ask questions, the biology students had the essential experience of free inquiry—the essence of the scientific method.

THE WRITING PROJECT AND THE METHODS COURSE

These brief examples of new teachers and more experienced teachers working together represent only a glimpse of what one local writing project site did to engage teachers. Other writing project sites created their own activities or techniques for regular meetings:

1. Reading and responding to related professional material
2. Watching videotapes of fellow teachers at work
3. Bringing students to a staff meeting and conferring with them publicly
4. Presenting the results of colleagues' visits to one another's room or combining classes to co-teach a writing workshop
5. Telling the story of a writer and his or her work and teasing out the implications for students
6. Brainstorming new teaching techniques, volunteering to try them out, and sharing results
7. Looking for one piece of student work prepared on an overhead projector and imagining how a conference with the student would go
8. Reading aloud children's literature and discussing how best to share it with students
9. Crafting mini-lessons and rehearsing its presentation with colleagues
10. Visiting other schools, attending conferences or workshops, and sharing observations and notes
11. Inviting guest speakers with expertise in a selected area of study
12. Inviting adults to work on their writing in order to closely understand techniques to be taught children
13. Collaborating on teaching plans for a new course of study
14. Presenting a new course of study, workshop tool, or classroom ritual to get feedback from colleagues (National Writing Project, 2003, p. 63)

Samuel Totten, Director of the Northwest Arkansas Writing Project, has also used the writing project model to create a course for teacher candidates that is specifically focused on the teaching of writing in content areas.

In "Writing to Learn for Preservice Teachers" Totten (2005) argues for a course dedicated to the teaching of writing that all teacher candidates would be required to take. The need for this course is not only made clear by examining the latest NAEP data, but as Totten argues, also by examining the overburdening of methods courses where the teaching of writing is supposed to occur. Often, method courses must provide instruction in everything from classroom management to learning theory which prevents the kind of practice, mentoring and feedback that are necessary for mastering complex material.

The course Totten (2005, p. 3) developed focuses on the writing-to-learn strategies that "can be used to facilitate learning of content, to deepen their understanding of what they are learning (e.g., issues, theories, concepts, events), and to foster thinking at increasingly higher levels (e.g., analysis, synthesis, and evaluation). He uses the foundations of the NWP's summer institute for teachers by first providing a rationale for incorporating writing that shows how it can improve overall learning. Next, through readings he provides an overview of process writing theory so that teacher candidates are conversant in theory and familiar with key practitioners. Finally, to present a wide variety of strategies, Totten brings to the class teacher-consultants representing a variety of subjects. He also provides teacher candidates with many opportunities to test out the strategies they are learning as well as offer ways to modify or revise them. By modeling his methods course after the NWP, Totten has provided teacher candidates with a sound foundation in theory and practice that will enable teacher candidates to take responsibility for their own professional development.

Alyson Whyte and Nancy Ellis have also reported on their use of the NWP model in the creation of a writing methods courses. In "The Power of Network Organization: A Model for School-University Collaboration" Whyte and Ellis (2004) demonstrate how the elements of the NWP's summer institute and the nature of the annual review process for NWP sites enhanced the dialogue between cooperating teachers in the schools, university instructors, and teacher candidates. While teacher candidates benefit from immersion in school settings throughout their course of study, Whyte and Ellis cited the many problems initiating, coordinating, and sustaining professional development schools that provide teacher candidates with these experiences. As an alternative to the professional development school, they experimented with using the network of schools and teachers associated with NWP. This eliminated the formal proposal and recognition processes required by school districts and universities to establish a partnership. Teacher candidates in the writing methods course devoted part of their time during the semester to observing and instructing in a school with a teacher who was also a writing project consultant. At regular intervals during the semester, the university instructor, cooperating teachers in the school, and the teacher candidates gathered to share and reflect both on theory and practice.

They concluded that two features of the NWP network led to increasing three-way communication among teacher candidates, teachers in the schools, and university instructors. The first feature of the NWP which fostered interaction was the extended time all the participants shared writing together, responding to self-chosen readings, and demonstrating best practices. These features are a hallmark of the 5-week invitational summer institute for teachers sponsored by the NWP. Through reading, writing, speaking, listening, and practicing, teachers from across all levels and all subjects learn to appreciate one another. By collaborating with teachers who attended the summer institute, Whyte and Ellis extended their writing methods course beyond the university classroom to engage teacher candidates in meaningful dialogue with practicing teachers.

Another feature the authors suggested aids in creating and sustaining communication is the NWP annual review process for each site within the national network. In a review process for funding that allows for variation in style and voice, the NWP institutionalizes shared decision-making and goal-setting that leads directly into operations. At each site leadership collaborates with teacher consultants to shape and revise their NWP site, and in its response to the application for funding, the NWP reinforces its overarching objectives by encouraging plans and programs that are manageable. The application for funding also requires garnering matching funds from leadership in the universities and local school communities. By gathering and extending the broadest possible base of support, the NWP institutionalizes the need for greater public dialogue about writing. Whyte and Ellis argue that the leadership of the NWP and its teachers show teacher candidates that they cannot teach in isolation, and that they will be at the forefront of shaping public attitudes toward writing and the teaching of writing.

IMPROVING THE TEACHING OF WRITING

The NWP could be even more involved in the preparation of writing teachers, but a paradigm shift needs to occur at the college and university level first. We must move away from the limited view of writing as a discrete subject area belonging just to specialists at the university level. Because writing can support a high level of learning in all core subjects, it matters in any classroom where inquiry, knowledge, and expression are valued and recognized by students and teachers. When teacher preparation programs harness writing as an essential tool for learning, they will give students the skills and confidence to be better writers and teachers of writing. Writing helps students become better readers and thinkers. It can help students reflect critically about the information and ideas they must understand in their content courses. As future teachers, they will help others to become participants and decision makers in a democratic society. This is why writing matters in the preparation of our teachers and the development of our new teachers.

REFERENCES

About the National Writing Project. (2005). Retrieved November 10, 2005, from www.writingproject.org/About.

Atwell, N. (1998). *In the middle: New understandings about writing, reading, and learning.* Portsmouth, NH: Heinemann Books.

Greenbuam C. A. (2002, March). *Classroom publication: Offering every student opportunities.* Presentation at the Louisiana State University Writing Project Spring Showcase, Baton Rouge, LA.

Greenwald, E.A., Persky, H.R., Campbell, J.R., & Mazzeo, J. (1999). *NAEP 1998 Writing report card for the nations and the states.* Washington, D.C.: National Center for Education Statistics, Office of Educational Research and Improvement, U.S. Department of Education. (NCES 482).

Hillocks, G. (1986). *Research on written composition.* Urbana, IL: National Conference on Research in English.

Jennings, C.D., & Hann, J. (2002). Why do I have to take remedial English? A collaborative model to solve a national problem. *Teaching writing in high school and college: Conversations and collaborations.* Urbana, IL: NCTE, 182–200.

National Center for Education Statistics. (1996). Can students benefit from process Writing? *NAEPfacts,* 1(3). Washington, DC: National Center for Education Statistics, Office of Educational Research and Improvement, U.S. Department of Education. (NCES 845).

National Commission on Writing in America's Schools and Colleges. (2003). *The neglected "R": The need for a writing revolution.* Princeton: College Entrance Examination Board.

National Writing Project. (2003). *Because writing matters: Improving student writing in our schools.* San Francisco: Jossey-Bass.

Totten, S. (2005). Writing to learn for preservice teachers. *The Quarterly,* 27(1),1–6.

Whyte, A., & Ellis, N. (2004). The power of a network organization: A model for school-university collaboration. *Contemporary Issues in Technology and Teacher Education,* 4(2), 137–151.

PART II

CLOSING GAPS IN THE WRITING CLASSROOM

CHAPTER 7

CLOSING THE GAP WITH CULTURALLY RELEVANT PEDAGOGY IN THE URBAN ENGLISH CLASSROOM

Patricia Ruggiano Schmidt and Kevin Salamone

ABSTRACT

This chapter describes the teaching/learning of one middle school English teacher who implemented culturally relevant pedagogy in seventh- and eighth-grade urban English classes. He made connections that closed the gap between the mandated state curriculum and students' interests and backgrounds to create lesson plans designed to motivate learning and develop classroom community. He came to understand that the success of his teaching appeared to relate to previous life experiences and information gained in a graduate literacy course.

A secondary middle school English teacher's implementation of culturally responsive literacy instruction brought immediate academic and social success in his classroom. So what is culturally responsive literacy instruction? This is instruction that makes connections with students' backgrounds/origins and interests/experiences to teach the required curriculum. Learning

Closing the Gap, pages 87–112
Copyright © 2007 by Information Age Publishing
All rights of reproduction in any form reserved.

becomes more relevant as teachers draw upon students' prior knowledge and experiences. And how can you tell it's happening in classrooms? Previous research in this area discovered seven key characteristics (Au, 1993; Boykin, 1978, 1984; Ladson-Billings, 1994, 1995; Moll, 1992; Osborne, 1996; Reyhner & Garcia, 1989; Schmidt, 2002, 2003, 2005). When lessons in secondary mathematics, social studies, science, language, and English content areas incorporate the seven characteristics, students stay more focused, become invested in what is happening, and actually step onto the road of academic success and social achievement (Tatum, 2000). Additionally, literacy development is promoted, since reading, writing, listening, speaking, and viewing provide the foundation for the seven characteristics of culturally responsive teaching (Schmidt, 2005). The seven characteristics are presented with brief definitions (Figure 7.1).

The project by an English teacher and a literacy professor that we describe in this chapter tells of a successful collaboration for the creation of culturally responsive lessons in a seventh- and eighth-grade urban setting. The two professionals worked together in the spring of 2005, as part of an independent study entitled, *Literacy Development across the Curriculum.* Additionally, secondary English teacher candidates were enrolled in a similar course taught by the professor in the same K–8 school. The candidates observed in classrooms, tutored students, and taught lessons in their specific content areas. Three candidates were placed in the English teacher's

---

1. **High Expectations**: supporting students as they develop the literacy appropriate to their ages and abilities.

2. **Positive relationships with families and community**: demonstrating clear connections with student families and communities in terms of curriculum content and relationships.

3. **Cultural sensitivity-reshaped curriculum**: mediated for culturally valued knowledge, connecting with the standards-based curriculum as well as individual students' cultural backgrounds.

4. **Active teaching methods**: involving students in a variety of reading, writing, listening, speaking, and viewing behaviors throughout the lesson plan.

5. **Teacher as facilitator**: presenting information, briefly-giving directions, summarizing responses, and working with small groups, pairs, and individuals.

6. **Student control of portions of the lesson**: the "healthy hum," talking at conversation level about the topic studied while completing assignments in small groups and pairs.

7. **Instruction around group and pairs**: low anxiety; completing assignments individually, but usually in small groups or pairs with time to share ideas and think critically about the work.

Figure 7.1.   Seven Characteristics for Culturally Responsive Instruction (Schmidt 2003).

seventh- and eighth-grade inclusive classes. The professor modeled lessons while the English teacher and the candidates observed. Then the English teacher designed and taught lessons observed by the professor and the candidates. Finally, the candidates designed and taught lessons while the professor, English teacher, and classmates observed. All regularly debriefed and reflected on the lessons, relishing in the many successful experiences.

The information gained from this project may contribute to teaching/learning successes in secondary schools where poverty issues and/or diverse ethnic and cultural backgrounds of students seem to contribute to academic failure. In this chapter, we (literacy professor Schmidt and English teacher Mr. Salamone) will first include a brief review of the research supporting culturally responsive teaching. Second, we will explain the college setting, the literacy course requirements and Mr. Salamone's independent study. Third, we will describe Mr. Salamone's classroom, school setting, curriculum, and summarize specific successful guided lessons. Finally, we will discuss the implementation of culturally responsive teaching in Mr. Salamone's seventh- and eighth-grade classroom.

WHY CULTURALLY RESPONSIVE INSTRUCTION?

Families and children from diverse ethnic and cultural backgrounds and lower socioeconomic levels often feel a discontinuity between home and school. When teachers reach out to connect with the interests of students, their family, and community members, there is often a narrowing of the academic gap and an increase in positive attitudes toward school (Au, 1993; Boykin, 1978, 1984; Edwards, 2004; Edwards et al., 1999; Faltis, 2000; Goldenberg, 1987; Heath, 1983; Ladson-Billings, 1995; Moll, 1992). The teachers who make this effort and create meaningful literacy lessons are actually implementing culturally relevant or culturally responsive pedagogy. These teachers connect the curriculum to the knowledge and experiences of diverse cultures in their classrooms by validating students' family backgrounds and using the literacies found in the students' cultures. For example, they recognize oral language expression, spacial relationship understandings, and mechanical abilities as well as many other examples of cultural literacies. Additionally, these teachers understand the culture of poverty and know how to relate to individuals and families by bridging their values to the dominant values of the middle class school culture (Payne, DeVol, & Smith, 2003). But, unfortunately, culturally knowledgeable teachers may be the exceptions in schools (Greene & Abt-Perkins, 2003; Nieto, 1999; Sleeter, 2001; Tatum, 2000). Therefore, teacher education programs have been called to the challenge of preparing teachers and administrators for culturally relevant or culturally responsive pedagogy as a means of promoting student academic achievement at all ages and stages of learning.

TEACHER EDUCATION PROGRAMS

Teacher education programs that use reading, writing, listening, viewing, and speaking to create consciousness-raising experiences actually help present and future teachers grasp a knowledge of self and others through autobiographies, biographies, reflection on diversity issues, and cross-cultural analysis (Cochran-Smith, 1995; Florio-Ruane, 1994; Noordhoff & Kleinfield, 1993; Osborne, 1996; Spindler & Spindler, 1987; Tatum, 1992; Willis & Meacham, 1997). However, those programs have not linked self-knowledge to teachers' implementation of home, school, and community connections for literacy instruction. Therefore, as a literacy professor, with 25 years of public school, classroom experience, I designed a model known as the *ABC's of Cultural Understanding and Communication* (Schmidt, 2001, 2002). I hoped that the model would contribute to teacher preparation and assist K–12, present and future teachers in connecting home, school, and community for literacy learning. Those who experience the ABC's Model write in-depth autobiographies, interview families of their students or someone from a different cultural background, and complete cross-cultural analyses. After this process, they begin designing lessons that are culturally relevant and make connections with community and family members.

Because of the success of the ABC's Model, many teacher education programs and teacher in-service programs have begun to use the model to develop the awareness that is fundamental to designing and implementing culturally responsive lessons (Finkbeiner & Koplin, 2002; Leftwich, 2002; Nagel, 2002; Schmidt, 1998, 1999, 2000, 2001, 2002, 2003, 2004; Xu, 2000a,b). Furthermore, the research from these programs are responsible for the discovery of *Seven Characteristics for Culturally Responsive Instruction* (Schmidt, 2003). Many of these characteristics emerged after I analyzed three years of participant observations and videotaped lessons across the curriculum in urban, high-poverty settings. As a result, teachers who become familiar with the characteristics refer to them when designing and evaluating their lessons. Similarly, Mr. Salamone and Professor Schmidt referred to them regularly during this project.

LITERACY PROFESSOR AND CULTURALLY RESPONSIVE LITERACY EDUCATION COURSES

I (the professor for the secondary literacy courses) am of European American origins and earned my doctorate at a local Northeastern university.

Presently, I teach in the graduate and undergraduate education programs at a small, liberal arts, religious affiliated college in the Northeast. Its 3000 undergraduate and graduate student populations are 90% European American from middle class backgrounds. About 10% of the students are from African American, Latino, Asian, Arabic, and Native American origins.

My doctoral dissertation analyzed the cultural conflicts and struggles of students from underrepresented populations in suburban classrooms. So, for the last 15 years, my research has focused on preparing teachers to make connections with their students and families through improved communication and culturally responsive literacy lessons. I designed the *ABC's of Cultural Understanding and Communication* as a process with the premise based on the adage, "Know thyself and understand others."

As a result of my work, the two literacy courses required for our state's secondary teacher certification programs deal directly with culturally relevant pedagogy. These courses help present and future secondary teachers understand the basics of the literacy development process, K–12, and set the stage for differentiating instruction across the curriculum. Key assignments for the two courses revolve around the *ABC's of Cultural Understanding and Communication* (Schmidt, 2001). I believe that teachers must first examine themselves personally before they begin the powerful task of assessing their students. Furthermore, after experiencing the ABC's Model, present and future teachers often find it more meaningful to design culturally responsive literacy lessons.

During the literacy courses, the graduate and undergraduate candidates also read numerous multicultural literacy sources, meet class guests from diverse cultural backgrounds, view *Teaching Tolerance Videos*, discuss diversity issues, debate numerous perspectives on differentiating instruction, role play stereotypes, and visit local cultural sites, such as places of worship, community centers, schools, neighborhoods, and community celebrations. Additionally, present and future teachers create and teach at least one culturally relevant content area lesson in a secondary school classroom. Throughout this process, I (the professor) act as facilitator for the courses; after a few sessions, dialogue both in and out of the classroom results in negotiations regarding syllabi foci and requirements. Similar to Freirean philosophy (1970), I am actually attempting to model the importance of getting to know students personally and professionally in the hope of meeting their needs. This perspective proves to be empowering: present and future teachers begin to see themselves controlling their own learning and many attempt this pedagogy in their present and future classrooms.

Typically, present and future teachers enrolled in the literacy courses observe the professor modeling lesson planning and implementation in the college classroom and, when possible, in the public school classroom, thus demonstrating how to apply course information. Candidates usually witness these literacy classes as positive learning settings. However, by the end of the coursework, there is a range of understanding concerning culturally responsive teaching. Some people actually change their thinking and begin to apply ideas immediately, while others begin to develop a greater awareness, but need more support to actually implement lessons. A few express concerns about the need for differentiating instruction for students from culturally and ethnically different backgrounds. In most cases, however, I find that these courses are positive learning experiences for all.

INDEPENDENT STUDY

During the spring of 2005, as I began teaching the undergraduate literacy course in an urban school setting, a seventh/eighth-grade English teacher (Mr. Salamone) requested that I facilitate an independent study for his graduate program. I agreed, seeing this as an opportunity to work on culturally relevant pedagogy in an authentic context. The population in this urban school is 44% African American, Latino, Asian and Native American students and 56% European American. There are approximately 760 students with 37% receiving free and reduced breakfasts and lunches. The school was a K–6 building for many years, but at the request of parents in the neighborhood it expanded to K–8. The structure is clean and well lit and was renovated to accommodate this expansion. The school sits in the center of an upper-middle-class neighborhood, borders on some of the city's high poverty areas, and draws children from both settings.

Three candidates observed and tutored in Mr. Salamone's classroom, as a major literacy course requirement. They saw lessons modeled by Mr. Salamone and me and then designed and implemented their own lessons.

To begin this independent study, Mr. Salamone and I analyzed my syllabus and tailored it to his needs and course requirements. We decided to meet before school and during his planning times to discuss readings and assignments. Mr. Salamone completed a modified ABC's Model, created and taught culturally responsive lessons, viewed videos and multicultural materials, perused multicultural literature, discussed literacy articles and text (Vacca & Vacca, 2005), and observed and evaluated our lessons and the candidates' culturally responsive lessons in his classroom. To better understand Mr. Salamone's classroom before the course and the changes he made during the course, it is important to read portions of his autobiography written for the *ABC's of Cultural Understanding and Communication* assignment.

MR. SALAMONE'S STORY

I grew up in Portland, Maine in the 1970s, which means I experienced very little cultural diversity in my youth. It's hard for me to remember the exact numbers, but my high school had approximately 600 students, only three of whom were African American and the only Latino was actually my best friend. He was half Irish. The rest of the school, as much as I can remember, included European American students, mostly from the Judeo/Christian traditions. My parents were teachers and very progressive thinkers in terms of diversity and tolerance. Hate was never taught in my household. Tolerance was held up as the highest of values. My parents, however, decided to reside in the predominantly white, middle-class, Portland, Maine. It was, after all, where my father grew up.

The Portland my father knew as a child was similar to mine in terms of racial diversity. However, he tells stories of how neighborhoods were divided along Euro-ethnic boundaries. How my grandfather, an Italian, was actually ostracized for marrying a Polish woman. Someone from the "other" neighborhood. I guess this could be a root of my father's progressive thinking.

My dad was also the first of his family to go to college. He attended New England Conservatory of Music, where he met my mother. I guess being musicians in Boston in the 1950s influenced their attitudes about tolerance. My dad also tells the story of how he met Martin Luther King, Jr. when he was in grad school. He attended Boston University for his Master's degree. It was there that he took singing lessons with Coretta Scott, back in the days when she was courting Martin Luther King. He met Martin several times as he came to pick up Coretta for dates after class. My dad also tells the story of how Martin Luther King spoke at his commencement ceremony. He was always proud of these stories, and that pride influenced me greatly.

Growing up, the only true diversity I ever experienced was through television. "The Jeffersons" and "Sanford and Son" were my only real interaction with African Americans. I, and everyone else in my school, never really interacted with people of other races. I also remember hearing friends of mine speaking in racist terms and demonstrating certain attitudes. However, I seldom saw anyone acting it out—person to person. There just wasn't enough diversity to actually see such things. I do remember that the few African American students at my school stuck together and only interacted with others through school activities. It was sad to watch. I can't imagine how isolated they must have felt.

It wasn't until I attended college that I gained experience in a diverse setting. In the classrooms, in intramural sports, in the cafeteria, I saw and experienced diversity first hand. I went to the University of Hartford in the early 1980s. This school recruited heavily from the New York City area. I saw nouveau-riche whites, urban blacks, Latinos, and Asians all interacting in a vibrant setting. I saw the good and the bad being acted out daily. I had African Americans living on my floor. We met in the dorm, in the classroom, but they, again, stuck together—afraid to truly mesh with the rest. And for good reason. I saw other whites actively excluding people based on their skin color or ethnic background. I did my best to stay in the middle and to take people as I saw them. My parents' influence spoke largely during this time of discovery.

After graduation, I spent seventeen years working mostly in the high tech business, in Boston, where racial diversity actually seemed healthy. Although I saw some discrimination, I must say that the company I worked for demonstrated a positive, inclusive philosophy. The lifeblood of the business depended on it. I can't imagine where that company would be without the contributions of people from so many walks of life.

Then, due to an interesting mid-life crisis, I found myself teaching. My first assignment was at an urban high school in a small Northeastern city as a Teaching Assistant/Substitute Teacher. On my first day, I walked in the main entrance and saw a line of students from many diverse ethnic and cultural backgrounds. At the front of the line was a group of teachers and administrators checking backpacks and students with metal detectors. I was introduced to the Vice Principal, who was himself working the line. I asked him where I should go first. He handed me a backpack and told me to look for weapons or drugs.

This was a long way from 1970s Portland, Maine. However, what a wonderful learning experience that assignment ended up being. This school displayed a wonderful commitment to cultural diversity. They had a multicultural fair where all the students created information booths representing some aspect of their cultural background. It was an amazing event. The food, music, dance, and art were wonderful. It was truly inspiring. A year at the high school then led to a full time job teaching middle school English in the same city district. I am in my second year of teaching English.

From his autobiography, it may be concluded that Mr. Salamone had a predisposition for teaching in an urban setting. He was raised to respect and appreciate differences. His life and work experiences seemed to reinforce these ideas. So, implementing what he was learning during the independent study seemed logical to him. His classroom and motivational materials indicated a desire to recognize cultural and linguistic differences even before the course began.

MR. SALAMONE'S CLASSROOM AND CURRICULUM

Mr. Salamone's classroom walls are covered with famous people and their words of wisdom from all continents and cultures. They are literary figures, musicians, athletes and historical leaders. The desks are arranged in a U shape and he constantly creates new seating charts with the philosophy that youngsters need to get to know the people in their classes. He begins each class with breathing exercises, something he thinks calms the hyper teens. He himself practices Yoga and believes that time spent settling down is essential for preparing students for the daily class agenda, always written on the blackboard. Mr. Salamone is proud of his classroom and expressed this in his own words.

> My classroom appears new. It is large, carpeted, and clean. I adorn the walls with posters of famous artwork, and a wall-length cartoon of Shakespeare. I've added posters of local African-American writers and quotes from people like Shakespeare, Andy Rooney, Muhammad Ali and Tupac Shakur. I've had the students engage in several art projects throughout the year and I hang their work alongside the other posters. I also have a board dedicated to all the A's earned on major projects throughout the year.
>
> We have block scheduling with ninety-minute classes. I see three sections of seventh graders one day, then I see eighth graders the next. There are twenty-eight students per class with the full range of academic and socioeconomic levels. My classes are bimodal. There are doctors' children sitting next to children who can't buy lunch, and children who read with great difficulty next to children who read with ease. I've taken workshops about differentiating instruction, and I study the needs of special students in graduate school, but I find much of the implementation challenging.
>
> I structure each ninety-minute class as a routine. I find the students take comfort in knowing what is going to come next. I start each class by reading the agenda off the board. We then begin with a brief, but important, breathing exercise. I am constantly amazed at how much stress the students bring to the classroom—from problems at home, to normal middle-school growing pains, to the raucous hallway. All of these stresses come billowing into my classroom each period. So, being a Yoga practitioner, I have the students breathe for five minutes. The students make fun of this at first, but soon grow to love the quiet time. It gets them to focus. I then have them read quietly for twenty minutes. I find I do not have enough copies of curriculum titles to go around for each student in each grade, so I have them read one book of their own choosing each month. I find that this is the only time many of my students ever read. I then have them journal.
>
> This consists of some thought-provoking prompt usually related to the day's lesson which I then discuss with them. I work hard to validate each of their responses during discussion, even when they are joking. I am always amazed, however, at their great responses. After these regular exercises, we launch into the daily lesson which varies from day to day. I have them reading and writing, of course, but I also try to engage the diversity of learning styles using art, music, games, and plays. I find that the extended time involved with a ninety-minute class is both a blessing and curse. Most students at this age do not have the attention span to last a full class, so I try hard to vary the lessons to maintain interest. With a shorter time, however, I would probably not be able to do the independent reading and journal.

I was given a curriculum based mostly on the New York State Academic Standards. To accomplish the breadth of requirements, I assign several books from the required list. We also read short stories and poetry from the text books supplied from the district and they write in as many styles as I can fit in the year: extended essays, poetry, plays, and short stories. I have discovered that each style brings out a different group of students. For instance, some students whom I could never seem to reach will shine when we do a poetry unit. I work hard to keep it relevant, interesting and fun.

Below is a rough curriculum map for my 2004–2005 year (dates are approximate). Journal and Independent Reading exercises are constant throughout the year:

Month	7th Grade	8th Grade
September	Community Building— Rules and Procedures Vocabulary Builders— Greek and Latin roots, context clues	Community Building— Rules and Procedures Vocabulary Builders— Greek and Latin roots, context clues
October	*The Outsiders*—Literary Elements (Characterization, Plot, Theme). Final essay and portfolio assessment.	*Call of the Wild*—Literary Elements (Characterization, Plot, Theme). Symbolism and deeper meanings.
November	Finish *The Outsiders*. *A Christmas Carol*—Focus on Characterization. Comparing movies and book. Journal Assessment	Finish *Call of the Wild*. Mini-Unit, Mark Twain. The author and his world. Journal Assessment
December	Finish *A Christmas Carol*	Finish Mark Twain. ELA, State Test Preparation— Extended Unit on test taking skills with review of terms and concepts. (test in early January)
January	I take 8th graders for most of month for test prep. "Exploration of Self" (study of short stories and poetry)	Test Preparation (cont.) Humor—The literary elements of humor (irony, buffoonery, etc.). Situational Comedy— Script writing and acting.
February	"Exploration of Self" (cont)—An in-depth exercise in essay writing. Poetry—The Blues. An exploration of blues music and poetry in celebration of Black History Month.	Poetry—The Blues. An exploration of blues music and poetry in celebration of Black History Month. Lyric writing and Kareoke. Underground Railroad
March	*Hatchet*—Guided Reading Practices. Interactive studies. The elements of the novel Journal Assessment	*So Far From the Bamboo Grove*— Guided Reading Practices. Interactive studies. The elements of the novel Journal Assessment

Month	7th Grade	8th Grade
April	*Hatchet* (cont.)—The students build their own study guides and teach a class. *Hatchet* Test (final assessment)	*So Far From the Bamboo Grove* (cont.)—Final Test for book.
May	Poetry and Mythology— Exploring elements of poetry along with oral tradition. Reciting poetry and storytelling. Café 303.	Science Fiction— Exploring the elements of science fiction. Film study.
June	Poetry and Mythology (cont.) Final Test Preparation	Science Fiction (cont.) Final Test Preparation

For a teacher in his second year, Mr. Salamone had created a learning environment with many excellent qualities, but he was anxious to learn more. He wanted better instruction for his students.

RATIONALE FOR THE INDEPENDENT STUDY

When Mr. Salamone and I first talked about the literacy course, he shared issues about classroom management, appropriate literature, and student comprehension and written expression. He had a genuine interest in his children's homes and cultures, but didn't know how to make connections for academic achievement. He talked of teaching *Call of the Wild* last fall but found that students had no interest in it. He recalled, "Class discussions were a waste and their writing was even worse." Mr. Salamone went into detail about the fall semester:

> In the semester previous to the independent literacy study, I taught *The Call of the Wild*. I diligently began building background, using some information about Jack London off the web. I drew some maps on the board to help them visualize the setting. I then jumped into the book. We did some round robin type reading. I'd read some chapters to them, and I would also have them listen to the book on tape. We did this all as a class with no grouping or pairing.

> Teaching this book was a painful experience. Being an urban school, I could not have picked a book that was further from their experience. Don't get me wrong, I feel it's important to open new worlds to students. That, to me, is the magic of reading. However, I did not do enough to build knowledge of the subject and allow them to engage in it. I literally stopped them from reading the book halfway through and showed some instructional videos I found on the web about the Klondike gold rush. I then had them draw some picture books to help them visualize the major scenes of the book. These measures salvaged the project. Many students slowly came around to the story.

Other problems involved Jack London's use of the language, which can be quite challenging for my eighth graders. I really didn't do enough vocabu-lary-building exercises to bolster their experience. I had them write an essay exploring certain themes brought out in the book. The essays were put together with their art work and story maps and passed in as a portfolio. The results were wide ranging with some surprising work, but most of it was medi-ocre at best.

Mr. Salamone seemed to understand adolescent behaviors. He incorpo-rated music and videos for instruction, and knew how to draw upon stu-dent interests. However, he did not know how to maintain student focus after he caught their interest. Therefore, while taking the literacy course, he worked on ways to build a strong knowledge foundation so students would read the assigned literature and think more critically about their studies. To better understand the significance of culturally responsive teaching, Mr. Salamone completed the *ABC's of Cultural Understanding and Communication*. He wrote his autobiography and informally told stories of the lives of his students. From that information, we discussed cross-cultural analyses and ways to make the curriculum relevant to students' lives.

In the next section, we will look at a summary of Mr. Salamone's progress in the course and examples of the resulting materials he created for his students.

MR. SALAMONE'S TEACHING/LEARNING: MULTICULTURAL LITERATURE, READING AND WRITING GUIDES

Multicultural Literature

The first strategy Mr. Salamone attempted was the use of multicultural literature as motivation for teaching units of study. He became familiar with authors such as Walter Dean Myers, Christopher Myers, Nikki Grimes, and Patricia McKissak and found that student discussions and comprehen-sion significantly increased.

Reading Guides

After creating guides and modeling their use in his classroom, Mr. Sala-mone was encouraged to create his own. First, he chose a trade book that would coincide with the social studies curriculum—*So Far From the Bamboo Grove*, a novel about the Japanese escaping from Korea toward the end of

World War II. It is the true story of a young Japanese girl named Ko who grew up in post-World War II Korea. It chronicles her escape from Korea to Japan and the hardship she endured with her family.

The unit began with a map study of Korea and Japan using a large Peter's Projection (1972) that had not previously existed in his classroom, but was analyzed during the literacy course. (It is a more accurate world map than those usually found in schools.) Students were able to see the U.S.A., Korea, and Japan in relation to one another, thus effectively situating the novel. He also invited an expert in Korean culture to talk about this era, as well as Korean life today. Students connected with artifacts brought into class by the guest through paired activities and lively discussions. Students also had relatives in the armed services and they talked about similar artifacts brought home as gifts. This experience set the stage for reading the novel.

Three-level guides created by Mr. Salamone assisted the students as they read chapters silently and in pairs, completing vocabulary and interpretive comprehension activities. Mr. Salamone circulated and worked with small groups and individuals having difficulties. The "healthy hum" prevailed as students read, listened, talked, and wrote together. Mr. Salamone gave them time for completing each part of the guide. He made sure to give less time than was needed to promote "staying on task." Those that finished early were given the choice to read ahead or complete short puzzle games or other related activities for the book.

Mr. Salamone was pleased with the results because he saw the students focused on reading, writing, listening, speaking, and viewing. At the end of the class, he found the summary discussions to be more critical and alive than before. The students had actually understood. He wrote few referrals to the office since students were completing the guides, sharing with their partners, and participating in whole group summaries. The special needs students were as active as the typical students, a new behavior not seen in previous classes. Mr. Salamone continued designing reading guides during the rest of the semester, all of which exemplified the *Seven Characteristics of Culturally Responsive Teaching*. The following are examples of three-level guides for reading in the eighth grade English class as explained by Mr. Salamone:

> I implemented the following guides by first using guided instructions for a focusing activity in front of the class. I then modeled, with the help of a student, how to complete a guide. I demonstrated how to alternate reading specific sections of the text aloud. The one not reading listened carefully for answers to questions. As students worked in pairs, I circulated, frequently stopping to help some students and to question others.

The following guide was tailored for a chapter that chronicled how Ko and her sister handled the death of their mother as well as some of her troubles with classmates.

Sample Reading Guide

Name: _____

Date: _____

So Far From the Bamboo Grove
Chapter 8

Class Discussion

This is a mess kit. (Show and pass around parts)

What things can you do with a mess kit?

Why do you think I wanted you to study a mess kit?

Directions: Write the page numbers that helped you find the answers. As you take turns reading, quietly aloud, with your partner answer the questions. Be sure to talk. Discuss your answers and be ready to share them in class. You will each hand in your reading guide at the end of class. What we do not finish today, we may continue tomorrow or finish as homework.

p. xx   What did Yoko want to do to the girl bullying her? What did she do instead?

p. xx   How did Yoko speak with the "trash man?" Why?

p. xx   Why did the trash man yell at the other girls?

p. xx   How did Yoko regard the "trash man?" She wanted to "talk with my

_____."

p. xx   Between Yoko and Ko, who got the most food and why?

p. xx   Why did Ko tell Yoko she had to go to school?

p. xx   What happened to the grand parents?

p. xx   What did mother tell Yoko to "hang on" to?

p. xx   What happened to Mother?

p. xx   How much did the men from the funeral service say the cremation would cost?

p. xx   What precious item did Ko take from mother's body?

p. xx   Who came to help Yoko and Ko? What was her name?

p. xx   How was the fire lit?

p. xx   How long did Ko say they had to stay in the city?

p. xx   What kind of factory did Mrs. Masuda own?

p. xx   What did Mrs. Masuda offer to Yoko and Ko?

p. xx   What did they use for an urn?

p. xx   What did the monk do?

p. xx   What "simple" thing did they make for mother?

p. xx   What did Yoko ask of mother?

Why do you suppose mother told Yoko to hold on to the blanket?

Why do you suppose Yoko and the trash man became friends?

With your partner, discuss how Yoko and Ko handled the funeral. What offerings did they give to Mother's urn? Discuss how this is similar or different from funerals you have experienced or heard about:

Extra Credit:

CALLIGRAPHY	COMMUNIST	CREMATION
HONORABLE	KOTO	KYOTO
MESSKIT	MRSMASUDA	SCHOOL
STREETCAR	SWORD	TRASHMAN

Search for the words and find the hidden message!

T	S	I	N	U	M	M	O	C	Y	E	O	L	K	O
N	K	T	O	A	H	I	D	T	L	E	O	Y	O	M
O	O	T	R	H	M	E	R	B	O	O	F	A	T	H
E	R	I	Y	E	H	H	A	M	H	K	Q	F	O	J
T	V	Z	T	N	E	R	S	C	E	N	M	H	P	U
E	R	V	E	A	O	T	S	A	I	S	R	A	N	E
Y	M	Y	Q	N	M	R	C	U	R	Y	S	K	Z	K
Z	D	Q	O	F	E	E	W	A	A	T	M	K	R	L
M	B	H	C	U	W	Q	R	F	R	A	A	Y	I	N
Y	W	U	F	C	U	Z	C	C	J	T	S	O	W	T
A	Z	C	K	D	V	I	L	Y	R	B	U	T	R	D
C	A	L	L	I	G	R	A	P	H	Y	D	O	R	D
Y	A	V	U	Q	G	M	Z	W	K	P	A	O	J	X
X	N	H	B	S	M	W	K	W	V	M	W	A	Y	Y
K	I	Z	J	Y	V	J	S	L	T	S	N	P	W	P

Mr. Salamone evaluated his guided lessons and saw that he had accomplished six of the seven characteristics of culturally responsive teaching. He was amazed at the successful completing of guides. The "healthy hum" in the classroom demonstrated that students could talk, listen, write, and share information. Students stayed on task and were ready for critical discussions. Mr. Salamone was free to roam the classroom facilitating individuals and pairs. However, he felt that community involvement was not as strong as it could have been. He had invited a community member in to discuss Korean culture, but next year he planned to systematically bring in Korean Americans who live in the community. He thought that he might invite one of the local funeral directors to discuss various cultural practices.

Mr. Salamone was so enthusiastic with the initial results that he continued creating guides for the next unit of study, *Hatchet*, by Gary Paulsen. With survival as the theme, the students responded with great interest to the fictional story of a boy who is forced to learn how to survive in the Canadian wilderness after a plane crash.

The following guide is structured for two chapters that describe the main character's struggles to find food and to build a fire. Mr. Salamone explained,

> I brought in and displayed camping supplies that would have helped the main character survive. Among the items were a backpack, a tarp, a gas-powered hiker's stove, a compass, a star chart, a mess kit, rope, and a sleeping bag. With a little help from me, several students constructed a lean-to with a tarp and set up a mini camp in the classroom.

Name: _____

Date: _____

Hatchet, Chapter 11 and 12

With your partner, choose three of the survival items and 3 different ways each could be used.

Item 1:
   Use 1:
   Use 2:
   Use 3:

Item 2:
   Use 1:
   Use 2:
   Use 3:

Item 3:
   Use 1:
   Use 2:
   Use 3:

Chapter 11

p. 103	What did Brian transfer from the beach to his shelter?
p. 104	What did Brian do to make his depression "leave?"
p. 104	How did Brian's see himself? What things did he see?
p. 105	What two things came together?
p. 106	What were Brian's plans for the signal fire?
p. 106	What type of bird did Brian see? What ideas did this bird give Brian?
p. 106	List six adjectives (describing words):
p. 108–109	Describe Brian's plans to catch this food?

Chapter 12

p. 110	Did Brian's plan work? Why or why not?
p. 111	How did Brian fix his mistakes? Did these fixes work?

p. 112	Do you like Brian's theory of how "primitive man" invented the bow and arrow? Do you agree with his theory? Explain.
p. 112	Why were the insects no longer bothering him?
p. 113	What made him hunt?
p. 114	What exploded at his feet?
p. 115	What did Brian hear?
p. 116	What happened to the sound?
p. 117	What was he sure of?
p. 117	Did Brian believe he could "make it?" Explain.

Finish the Cause and Effect diagrams below:

"Discoveries happened because they needed to happen." In what ways is Brian learning this concept?

On page 105, Brian believes he was actually "seeing" things rather than "noticing" them. What does he mean by this?

How has Brian changed? Read pages 105–107 for ideas.

Mr. Salamone's students were so successful with the guides that he tried a radical idea. He showed groups of students how to write their own guides and teach the class. His high expectations for his students' creative abilities and positive academic behaviors translated into writing and teaching activities that had a real impact on the class. Here are two examples of how Mr. Salamone helped students teach their classmates:

Team Members: _____ , _____ .

_____ , _____

Date: _____

Hatchet—Creating a Lesson Plan

Teaching involves more than just handing out a worksheet and making sure the students are on task. You need to take attendance. You need to set up procedures (When do students pass in their work? Where do they hand the work in? How do you want the class organized? How will you handle passes?)

Here are the things you need to do . . .

Attendance—Have one team member take attendance. Each absence needs to be marked with a slash. Tardies are marked with another slash. Attendance must be placed in the folder outside the door within the first 20 minutes.

Your attendance taker is: _____

Breathing—It is a part of class. All students must have their eyes shut and relaxing. One student will lead this.

Your breathing leader is: _____

Independent Reading—Each student must participate. There will be one student making sure students are on task. Mr. Salamone will be helping with most of this. One student will be in charge of coordinating bathroom breaks and passes. One at a time.

Your Independent Reading Coordinator is: _____

(Note: It's expected that you read during this activity).

Journal—The journal needs to reflect the lesson of the day. Pick a team member who will explain the journal. Decide if you want this journal to be part of the guide or to be put in the students' regular journal.

Your Journal Coordinator is: _____

The Lesson—You need to have the students work on your chapter using the guide you wrote. However, you can add a game or some fun activity to enhance the learning. The game and/or the activity, however, needs to be relevant to the lesson (i.e., you can't just play 7-Up for the sake of playing). You can use art or any other activity you may want.

All of you will be involved in delivering the lesson.

Answer the following . . .

The Objectives: What do want your students to learn from your lesson? (Think of any general knowledge, vocabulary, or other concepts you want them to learn.)

The objective of our lesson is: _____

Materials: What materials will the students need to finish your activity? (Don't forget the details.) Materials for this lesson include: _____

_____

Procedures: What will you have the students do first, second, third, etc.? (Don't forget the details.)

Activity 1:

Activity 2:

Activity 3:

Activity 4:

Activity 5:

Assessment: How do you know your students learned what you wanted them to learn? Will you quiz them? (You'll need to write one.) Will you run a classroom discussion? I will assess my students in the following way (describe in full sentences):

By teaching the young people how to create guides, Mr. Salamone helped them study and learn the material. Here is his template for the students:

Group members: _____ , _____ ,

_____ , _____

Create Your Own *Hatchet* Study Guide

Chapter:

1. Read the chapter with your partner.

2. Think of a focusing question, journal prompt, or focusing activity. Think of what happened in the chapter. You want your class to focus on the main idea. If you decide on a journal prompt, write a question or prompt that will help them focus. If you decide on an activity (a show-and-tell related to the chapter or some sort of demonstration), then write your idea below.

Write your prompt or idea here:

3. Go page by page and write down at least one question for each. You want the student to think about what is happening in the story. You want to cover each page with at least one question.

p. _____ Q:

p. _____ Q:

p. _____ Q:

p. _____ Q: etc.

4. Create a crossword puzzle or word search on the back of this sheet. Include at least 8 words.

5. Ask at least two short answer questions. You have to get your students to think about the main points in the chapter.

Question 1:

Question 2:

Question 3:

EVALUATION

Mr. Salamone was encouraged by students' work on the reading guides. There was a "healthy hum" and active involvement. He saw students reading and comprehending as they shared in pairs. He lost his anxious feelings related to control as he observed students reading, writing, and discussing literature in critical ways. Previous to the literacy independent study, he would not have thought to bring in community members, but he saw how positive the experience was for his students to meet experts on Korea. He realized the necessity of building on prior knowledge and that the time spent was important to the understanding and appreciation of reading materials. Mr. Salamone even became confident enough to invite his students to create and teach guides for short stories and poetry. This evolved into a memorable learning experience for the students. Typical of their responses were the following:

"Hey, it's hard to teach!"

"Some of the kids can be pains."

"You have to decide what's important when you teach."

"They have to pay attention and you gotta get 'em to do it."

"I liked it, but I don't know if I want to do it again."

Mr. Salamone let go to gain control of his classroom and the students were empowered to take control of their own learning. He was enthused about next year because of his success.

WRITING GUIDES—ESSAY FOR UNIT ONE

The first unit in the seventh-grade English text offered several short stories by authors from diverse backgrounds: Langston Hughes, Julia Alvarez, Chaim Potok, Gary Soto and Cynthia Rylant. Each story involves the concept of possession (gift giving, names, wanting something you can't get, etc.). After the students studied these stories, they wrote a 400-word essay about their favorite possessions and delivered short presentations to the class about the possessions. Some students chose their names as a favorite possession. One student explained that her name, Yorel, was actually her father's name backwards (Leroy). Another student brought in a beautiful quilt she sewed with her grandmother in Maine. Each patch represented something she had done with her grandmother in the out-of-doors. Here is an example of a successful guide:

Name: _____

Date: _____

Essay for Unit One

Personal possessions, both material and immaterial, play a big part in several stories we've read so far. In *Thank You, M'am*, Roger tries to steal Mrs. Jones' purse to buy a pair of suede shoes. In turn, he learns some valuable life lessons. In *Names, Nombres*, Julia speaks of her own name as an important possession. She discusses how it helped form her identity as she grew up. Both *Zebra* and *A Crush* discuss the importance of giving. Zebra created a helicopter out of discarded items and gave it to Mr. Wilson. Ernie gives Dolores flowers, which helps them both gain some self esteem.

You are to write a 400-word essay about a personal possession that is important to you. Like Roger, it could be something you really wanted but never really got. Like Julia, it could be something simple like your name. Like Zebra or Ernie, it could be something you gave to someone else. In the essay, make sure to cover the following:

How did you get this possession?

Describe it in as much detail as you can (if it is your name, tell how you got the name).

Explain why it is so important to you.

Make sure to discuss one of the stories we've read in this unit. You can do this in any way you wish. You can use quotes, cite examples for comparison, etc.

Additionally, you will be asked to either bring in this item or bring in a picture of it (You can draw it if you want to). You will also be asked to discuss this item in front of the class.

The first draft is due: _____

The final draft is due: _____

We will be using a series of in-class workshops to write this essay over the next few days. Take full advantage of this class time. The rubric appears on the back of this sheet.

THE WORDS OF THE GREAT POETS BECOME OUR OWN

A poetry project was another example of culturally responsive teaching. Several class periods were spent studying the elements of poetry. Students read as many poems as possible by authors from diverse backgrounds: Asian Haiku, Rap (Tupac Shakur), Irish (Seamus Heaney), and Latin-American (Martin Espada). Then, large print copies of each poem (about 20 in all) were placed around the room. The students chose copies of at least four poems. They then cut out each word from each poem, resulting in a pile of words in front of the small group. They then created a poem using these words and pasted the poem on decorated construction paper. This idea came from a documentary about Pop Star, David Bowie. Students were fascinated with the whole procedure and seemed to lose their fear of writing and reading poetry. A simple guide for their work was all that was needed to inspire and keep them on track to produce poetry throughout the year.

The Blues/Poetry Project

Another writing project involved exposing students to a vast array of blues songs and poetry. This required teacher research since many blues songs are repetitive and do not have much to offer in terms of teaching poetry elements (rhyming, alliteration, etc.). Students learned of the history of Blues, listened to songs, and studied the lyrics. In groups, they wrote their own Blues songs and performed on a Kareoke machine brought into the classroom. The following guide facilitated the project:

Name (give yourself a Blues nickname): ....

Names of Team Members (include Blues nicknames): .... ,

.... , ...

30 points

Your group has the blues, and the best way to chase them away is to sing. Your job will be to write and perform a Blues song. On the other side of this worksheet is an example of a Blues song that "Greased Lightnin'" Salamone wrote which goes to the tune on the Kareoke machine. Now, 'ole "Greased Lightnin'" would like to see some of you sing and others of you make a poster depicting your song. Understand that someone, however, needs to perform the song in front of the class. Someone needs to write the song, and someone needs to do the artwork. How you divide up the work is up to you, but everyone needs to work.

Step 1: You need to write a Blues song. Note the example on the back of this worksheet. It consists of 6 lines per verse: two repeated couplets followed by two more lines which rhyme with the first and third. The tune on the Kareoke machine allows for two verses, a guitar solo, and one last verse. So, you need to write three verses in all. What do you write about? Anything that gives you the blues—school, homework, nagging parents, Mr. Salamone—anything, as long as it is appropriate for the classroom and does not make anyone feel uncomfortable. Make sure, however, that there is a theme. It does not have to be serious, but you do need a theme.

Step 2: You need to create a poster that will provide a visual backdrop for your song. If you're singing about homework, draw a student pulling his or her hair out in front of a big stack of books. The poster needs to be colorful and well thought out.

Step 3: You will need to pass in your work. I will want a legible copy of your song and the art work. I also want you to fill out the "Blues" crossword puzzle with a "Student Reflection" written out on the back. You will be graded according to the following rubric:

Content: Did a lot of thought go into the song? Did you follow the format? Did you include a theme?

1   2   3   4   5

Performance: I understand you are not all fantastic musicians. What I am looking for, however, is teamwork and effort. Everyone should play a role. Those who work will **not** be penalized by those who do not. I watch and know who does the work.

1   2   3   4   5

Artwork: Was it well thought out and appropriate to your theme?

1   2   3   4   5

Student Reflection: Did the student fill out the student reflection completely? Did the student outline his or her role on the team? Was it evident that the student helped?

1   2   3   4   5

Mr. Salamone provided a model for the students regarding Blues poetry. His Blues poem sums up his fears and joys of teaching the English Language Arts. The students appreciated his effort.

Those Low Down, Good for Nuthin, Teachin' ELA at Roberts Blues
By "Greased Lightnin" Salamone

I've got those teachin' ELA blues
got you learnin' to read and write
I've got those teachin' ELA blues
got you learnin' to read and write.
But then you say, "I don't know nuthin"
And I say . . . you know, that can't be right.

Well I came to teach on Monday . . .
I did not know what to do.
Well I . . . came in to teach on Monday
I did not know what to do
I thought you'd like Jack London
and you just said, no that won't do.

I got vocab, and grammar rules
I got you readin' and writin' all the time.
I got vocab, and grammar rules
I got you readin' and writin' all the time
I've got you independent readin' and talkin' and
you just learn somethin' all the time.

PLANS FOR NEXT YEAR

Mr. Salamone had specific plans for the following year:

> Next year, I will focus on getting more community and parental involvement. First, I have an unusually large workload in terms of numbers. I find it very difficult to get a handle on the skill levels and needs of each of my students. To help better connect with my students, I will be scheduling individual meetings that will occur outside of class time. My principal was open to scheduling a substitute teacher for a number of afternoons so I can conduct these meetings. These meetings will involve a review of the students' writing and performance on tests along with some strategizing for future improvement. Parents will be invited to these meetings. I also plan to invite parents and other community members in to speak and even read to the class. Having a community member discuss her knowledge of Korea provided a wonderful scaffolding experience for the book *So Far From the Bamboo Grove*. I will be seeking more of these activities.

CONCLUSION

Obviously, Mr. Salamone was predisposed to culturally responsive teaching. We may conclude that this is why he met with success, but how many other predisposed teachers in urban classrooms have not received literacy methods preparation? How disheartening for them to not have the information and support necessary to reach out and connect successfully to make learning relevant for our young. How many of those teachers will we lose in frustration? Our best teachers? Mr. Salamone leaves us with a strong statement for teacher preparation and professional development:

> Using the guided reading/writing techniques made a huge impact on my classroom (Vacca & Vacca, 2005). The independent study was a great way to learn. Before this course, I had very few methods courses and little experience with culturally relevant content or lesson planning. The guided reading/ writing techniques are wonderful ways to not only teach novels and basic writing and poetry, but also to see that they will help me develop classroom management at the beginning of the school year. Prepared teachers can help students make connections with any book or document, no matter what their reading or writing levels. I also found that I like to circulate in the classroom. I get to know the students and they feel more comfortable asking me for help "on the sly" if I am close by and just under the pitch of the "healthy hum." My connections with them were enhanced, and their connections with the material were enhanced. We all won!

REFERENCES

Arno, P. (1972). *Peter's projection world map.* Amherst, MA: ODT, Inc.

Au, K. (1993). *Literacy instruction in multicultural settings.* New York: Harcourt, Brace Javanovich College Publishers.

Boykin, A,W. (1984).Reading Achievement and the social-cultural frame of reference of Afro-American children. *Journal of Negro Education 53*(4), 464–473.

Boykin, A,W. (1978). Psychological/behavioral verve in academic/task performance: Pre-theoretical considerations. *Journal of Negro Education, 47*(4), 343–354.

Cochran-Smith, M. (1995). Uncertain allies: Understanding the boundaries of race and teaching. *Harvard Educational Review 65* (4), 541–570.

Edwards, P. A. (2004). *Children's literacy development: Making it happen through school, family, and community involvement.* Boston, MA: Allyn & Bacon.

Edwards, P.A., Pleasants, H., & Franklin, S. (1999). *A path to follow: Learning to listen.*

Faltis, C. J. (1993; 2000). *Joinfostering:* Adapting teaching strategies for the multilingual classroom. New York: Maxwell Macmillan International.

Finkbeiner, C. & Koplin, C. (2002). A cooperative approach for facilitating intercultural education. *Reading Online, 6*(3). Newark, DE: International Reading Association.

Florio-Ruane, S. (1994). The future teachers' autobiography club: Preparing educators to support learning in culturally diverse classrooms. *English Education, 26* (1), 52–56.

Freire, P. (1970). Pedagogy of the oppressed. (M.B. Ramos, Trans.). New York: Seabury.

Goldenberg, C. N. (1987). Low-income Hispanic parents' contributions to their first-grade children's word-recognition skills. *Anthropology and Education Quarterly,18,* 149–179.

Greene, S., & Abt-Perkins, D. (2003). *Making race visible: Literacy research for cultural understanding.* New York: Teachers College Press.

Heath, S. B. (1983). *Ways with words: Language life and work in communities and classrooms.* Cambridge, UK: Cambridge University Press.

Igoa, C. (1995). *The inner world of the immigrant student.* Mahwah, NJ: Lawrence Erlbaum Associates, Inc.

Ladson-Billings, G. (1994). *The dreamkeepers: Successful teachers of African American children.* San Francisco, CA: Jossey-Bass.

Ladson-Billings, G. (1995). Culturally relevant teaching. *Research Journal, 32*(3), 465–491.

Leftwich, S. (2002). Learning to use diverse children's literature in the classroom: A model for preservice teacher education. Reading Online,V6(2). MACROBUTTON HtmlResAnchor www.readingonline.org: International Reading Association.

Moll, L.C. (1992). Bilingual classroom studies and community analysis: Recent trends. *Educational Researcher, 21*(2), 20–24.

Nagel, G. (2002). Building cultural understanding and communication: A model in seven situations. *Reading Online,* V6(4). MACROBUTTON HtmlResAnchor www.readingonline.org: International Reading Association.

Nieto, S. (1999). *The light in their eyes.* New York: Teachers College Press.

Noordhoff, K., & Kleinfield, J. (1993). Preparing teachers for multicultural classrooms. Teaching and *Teacher Education, 9*(1), 27–39.

Osborne, A. B. (1996). Practice into theory into practice: Culturally relevant pedagogy for students we have marginalized and normalized. *Anthropology and Education Quarterly, 27*(3), 285–314.

Payne, R., DeVol, P., & Smith, T.D. (2003). *Bridges out of poverty: Strategies for professionals and communities.* New York: Aha Press, Inc.

Reyhner, J., & Garcia, R. L. (1989). Helping minorities read better: Problems and promises. *Reading Research and Instruction, 28* (3), 84–91.

Schmidt, P.R. (1998). The ABC's Model: Teachers connect home and school. In T. Shanahan & F.V. Rodriguez-Brown (Eds.), *National reading conference yearbook 47* (pp. 194–208.) Chicago: National Reading Conference.

Schmidt, P. R. (1999). Know thyself and understand others. *Language Arts, 76,*(4), 332–340.

Schmidt, P.R. (2000). Teachers connecting and communicating with families for literacy development. In T. Shanahan & F.V. Rodriguez-Brown (Eds.), *National reading conference yearbook 49* (pp. 194–208.) Chicago: National Reading Conference.

Schmidt, P.R. (2001). The power to empower. In P.R. Schmidt and P.B. Mosenthal (Eds.). *Reconceptualizing literacy in the new age of multiculturalism and pluralism.* Greenwich,CT: Information Age Press.

Schmidt, P. R. (2002). *Cultural conflict and struggle: Literacy learning in a kindergarten program.* New York: Peter Lang.

Schmidt, P.R. (2003). *Culturally relevant pedagogy: A study of successful in-service.* Paper presented at the annual meeting of the National Reading Conference, Scottsdale, AZ.

Schmidt, P.R. (2005). *Preparing educators to communicate and connect with families and communities.* Greenwich, CN: Information Age Publishing.

Sleeter, C. E. (2001). Preparing teachers for culturally diverse schools. *Journal of Teacher Education, 52*(2), 94–106.

Spindler, G., & Spindler, L. (1987). *The interpretive ethnography of education: At home and abroad.* Hillsdale, NJ: Lawrence Erlbaum Associates.

Tatum, A. (2000). Breaking down barriers that disenfranchise African American adolescent readers in low-level tracks. In P. Mason & J S. Schumm, Eds., *Promising practices for urban reading instruction* (98–118), Newark, DE: International Reading Association.

Tatum, B. (1992). Talking about race, learning about racism: The application of racial identity theory in the classroom. *Harvard Educational Review, 62*(1), 1–24.

Teaching Tolerance Videos (1991–2003). 4000 Washington Avenue, Montgomery, AL 36104.

Vacca, R.T. & Vacca, J.L. (2005). *Content area reading: Literacy and learning across the curriculum* (8th Ed.). Boston: Pearson.

Willis, A.I. & Meacham, S.J. (1997). Break point: The challenges of teaching multicultural education courses. *JAEPL, 2,* 40–49.

Xu, H. (2000a). Preservice teachers integrate understandings of diversity into literacy instruction: An adaptation of the ABC's Model. *Journal of Teacher Education, 51*(2), 135–142.

Xu, H. (2000b). Preservice teachers in a literacy methods course consider issues of diversity. *Journal of Literacy Research, 32*(4), 505–531.

Novels Cited

London, J. (2003). *Call of the wild.* San Francisco, CA: Aladdin.

Paulsen, G. (1999). *Hatchet.* New York: Simon Pulse.

Watkins, Y. (2000). *So far from the bamboo grove.* San Francisco, CA: Sagebrush.

CHAPTER 8

"I KNOW I CAN
BE WHAT I WANT TO BE"

Using Rap Lyrics to Encourage
Self-Reflection and Meaningful Writing
from Students of Color

Karen Keaton Jackson

ABSTRACT

Many Composition scholars suggest that we can better embrace students' identities and literacy practices by implementing a culturally relevant pedagogy where they question traditional ideologies and analyze both themselves and the world around them. Yet, in a school system with so many federal and state mandated objectives, assignments, and course readings, how can we successfully implement a culturally relevant pedagogy full of non-mainstream materials and activities in a secondary English classroom? How can we, in good conscience, allow students to express their home experiences, including their home dialects, in the writing classroom when we know that Standard English is privileged in our educational system and in society? In other words, how can we best close the gaps between students' home literacy practices and school writing expectations? In this chapter, I describe a culturally

Closing the Gap, pages 113–127
Copyright © 2007 by Information Age Publishing
All rights of reproduction in any form reserved.

relevant writing assignment I performed with African-American middle school students that draws on their home identities and also encourages them to think critically about society and the role they want to play in it. Through culturally sensitive assignments such as the one analyzed here, teachers can encourage quality writing from students in a way that is inclusive of their own experiences while also preparing them for larger society.

While there are some educators who firmly believe that "good writing is good writing," and that students must attain such a level of writing no matter what the cost, a large number of writing teachers believe in the value of acknowledging and embracing students' feelings about literacy and writing instruction. When teaching writing and, more specifically, when teaching writing to students of color, concern for the affective component of learning becomes even more critical. According to many current Compositionists—Geneva Smitherman (1977), Keith Gilyard (1991, 1996), Victor Villanueva (1993) and others—teachers need to realize that for many students of color, literacy practices (which may not be Standard English) are tied to their racial, cultural, and communal identities. Yet often, the "good writing" that many teachers want their students to produce contradicts and silences students' native way of communicating.

If we accept the challenge that current Composition theory presents to us, we must learn to respect students' home identities, realizing that their literacy practices are inexplicably tied to those identities. Many scholars suggest that we can better embrace students' identities and literacy practices by implementing a culturally relevant pedagogy where they question traditional ideologies and analyze both themselves and the world around them. A culturally relevant pedagogy is a critical approach that gives students space to be active learners, tap into their own experiences, and use their own voices to make new meaning. This pedagogy calls for a variety of assignments, many of which are non-traditional in terms of content and form. More specifically for African-American students, culturally relevant teaching allows students to pursue academic success and simultaneously identify with their racial and cultural communities.

Though the idea of a culturally relevant pedagogy sounds wonderful in theory, there are several practical concerns that come to mind. In a school system with so many federal and state mandated objectives, assignments, and course readings, how can we successfully implement a culturally relevant pedagogy full of non-mainstream materials and activities in a secondary English classroom? How can we, in good conscience, allow students to express their home experiences, including their home dialects, in the writing classroom when we know that Standard English is privileged in our educational system and in society? In other words, how can we best close the gaps between students' home literacy practices and school writing expectations?

In order to explore some of these concerns, I describe and analyze a culturally relevant reading and writing assignment I performed with African-American middle school students that draws on their home identities and also encourages them to think critically about society and the role they want to play in it. Through culturally sensitive assignments such as the one analyzed here, teachers can encourage quality writing from students in a way that is inclusive of their own experiences while also preparing them for larger society.

THE LINK BETWEEN LITERACY AND RACIAL IDENTITY

To establish a context for my culturally relevant writing assignment, I first must review the research that explores the link between literacy and racial identity. Historically, our nation always has linked one's intelligence with one's ability to communicate in Standard English. Thus, if one had not mastered the Standard dialect—which often was the case for African Americans who were more likely than Whites to come from lower socioeconomic backgrounds—one was not seen as intelligent. However, as the Civil Rights movement developed in the 1960s and 1970s, more scholars of color emerged, arguing for the validity of nonstandard dialects, specifically the African American Vernacular. They claimed that for many African Americans, the vernacular is not just the means for expressing their identities, but actually is a part of their identities.

Well-known scholar and educator Geneva Smitherman (1977) traces the history, structure, and functions of the African American Vernacular of English (AAVE) in her text *Talkin' and Testifying: The Language of Black America*. In this work, Smitherman claims that the dialect is inseparable from its speaker's identity and culture:

> In a nutshell: Black Dialect is an Africanized form of English reflecting Black America's linguistic-cultural African heritage and the conditions of servitude, oppression, and life in America . . . Black English . . . is a combination of language and style interwoven with and inextricable from Afro-American culture. (pp. 2–3)

This intimate connection between language and identity demonstrates the emotional component of literacy instruction. Smitherman goes on to cite Frantz Fanon who says "Every dialect is a way of thinking" (p. 171). In other words, one does not use dialect only to express ideas; it is the medium through which one processes and creates new knowledge. When students compose, then, they are not merely writing random words, but rather are using carefully chosen words and sentence structures to help them think through ideas and express themselves.

Two years later, in 1979, researcher and writer James Baldwin entered the discussion on African-American students and their literacy practices in his article, "If Black English Isn't a Language, Then Tell Me, What Is?" Baldwin (1998/1979) begins by noting the close relationship between literacy and its speaker:

> Language, incontestably, reveals the speaker... It is the most vivid and crucial key to identity. It reveals the private identity, and connects one with, or divorces one from, the larger public, or communal identity. (pp. 67–68)

Here, Baldwin illustrates the power of language to confirm one's personal identity and connection to one's race, or to suppress and deny one's identity when that power is misused. Within this quote, Baldwin also shows that through literacy choices, young African-American students are making huge decisions about with whom they accept or identify themselves, whether it is the Black community through the African American Vernacular, or mainstream society through Standard English.

Pennsylvania State University professor Keith Gilyard (1991) illustrates Baldwin's claim about the struggle between identities in his autobiographical text *Voices of the Self: A Study of Language Competence*. He recalls how, while growing up, he created semi-selves—one self or identity to cope with academic life, and another self that coped with street life. While he was "Raymond," he spoke Standard English and performed well in his honors courses; while he was "Keith," he spoke the African American Vernacular and related easily to his African-American friends on the street (p. 43). In other words, he makes explicit the connection between his identities with the literacy practices he used while enacting certain behaviors. Neither the identity nor the voice would make sense without the other.

Gilyard goes on to note that his "linguistic role-playing" was not as easy as it may have appeared. As he got older, it became more difficult to keep "Keith" and "Raymond" separate. Gilyard felt that he could show no signs of streetwise "Keith" when in the honors classroom, and no evidence of academically successful "Raymond" when with his African-American neighborhood friends. He suffered a great deal psychologically and emotionally as he tried to maintain his two selves. Ultimately, he argues that no student should have to struggle as he did. He wanted to maintain his African-American identity and relationships, yet he also wanted to be successful in larger society. Unfortunately, in the rough neighborhood where he was raised, he rarely saw evidence that both goals—a positive racial identity and mainstream success—could be achieved.

The claims shown by Smitherman, Baldwin, Gilyard and others strongly urge writing teachers to see the need for respecting the link between language and identity. In his autobiography *Bootstraps: From an American Academic of Color*, researcher and scholar Victor Villanueva (1993) begins with the premise that language and identity are connected and that forms of "internal colonialism" operate in our society and educational system through literacy (pp. xii, xvi). According to Villanueva, society currently treats the minority problem as an immigrant problem. The mindset is that "once there are two generations that learn standard English, they will be...all better" (p. 19). But, Villanueva points out that African Americans lost their native tongue hundreds of years ago, and the discrimination has not disappeared.

Research shows that in the past, and present, writing teachers do not honor diverse dialects, which translates into them not respecting the *speakers* of those dialects, either:

> Research on language attitudes consistently indicates that teachers believe African American English-speaking children are 'nonverbal' and possess limited vocabularies. Speakers of African American English are often perceived to be slow learners or uneducable: their speech is often considered to be unsystematic and in need of constant correction and improvement. (Ball & Lardner, 1997, p. 472)

Because of these misconceptions, Ball and Lardner go on to call for teacher-sensitivity training and teacher awareness regarding the African American Vernacular and those who speak it. Particularly, they argue that the teacher, the student, and the site of literacy instruction should influence each other in dialogical relationships, and that we must find ways to turn barriers into bridges between home language and school language.

CULTURALLY RELEVANT TEACHING

Former public school teacher and current professor Gloria Ladson-Billings believes teachers can best embrace African-American students' identities by implementing a culturally relevant pedagogy:

> The primary aim of culturally relevant teaching is to assist in the development of a "relevant black personality" that allows African American students to choose academic excellence yet still identify with African and African American culture. Specifically, culturally relevant teaching is a pedagogy that empowers students intellectually, socially, emotionally, and politically by using cultural referents to impart knowledge, skills, and attitudes. These cultural

referents are not merely vehicles for bridging or explaining the dominant culture; they are aspects of the curriculum in their own right. (pp. 17–18)

A culturally relevant pedagogy eliminates the division of self Keith Gilyard speaks of, for in a classroom where a teacher uses this approach, students will feel comfortable excelling without feeling that their racial identity is being threatened. With a culturally relevant approach, teachers are to view knowledge critically, to see excellence as "a complex standard [that]...takes student diversity and individual differences into account" (Ladson-Billings, 1994, p. 81), to see teaching "as pulling knowledge out," which assumes students already possess intelligence, and to help "students make connections between their community, national, and global identities" (p. 34).

By nature of its non-traditional goals, a culturally relevant pedagogy will require teachers to go outside of traditional textbooks, assignments, and methods. Because of the additional time and resources required, many teachers, for good reason, may question how realistic it may be to implement such a curriculum. Teachers find themselves pressed for time with the curriculum as it is. As a result, many educators may shy away from adding supplemental work, fearing that students may perform poorly on standardized tests and in subsequent grades if they do not master the basic requirements. Yet, when teachers plan carefully and considerately, they can create writing assignments that allow students to see themselves represented in the materials and learn the skills necessary for success in the larger society.

THE NAS LESSON: A CULTURALLY RELEVANT PEDAGOGY IN ACTION

Recently, I had the opportunity to perform a culturally relevant lesson with a group of middle school students in a language arts classroom in Detroit, Michigan. The school is populated with nearly five hundred sixth-to-eighth grade students, 99% of them African American and 61% of them considered "at-risk" either academically or socioeconomically. Though the students were required to adhere to a dress code each day, their African-American identities came through consistently. Out of a class of twenty-eight students, six of the students, boys and girls, had either African braids or cornrows (most recently made popular by athletes such as Allen Iverson and countless other entertainers) and four of the boys had Afros.

In both content and style, students' literacy practices heavily reflected their African American identities. The class in which I worked was 100% African American and nearly all of the students spoke the African American Vernacular at least some of the time, particularly as they conversed and joked with each other (whether they were playing the "dozens" or rapping a popular hip-hop song).

My objectives for the lesson were for students to do the following: (1) Perform a close, critical reading of song lyrics; (2) Clearly communicate their opinions about the message of the song; (3) Engage in critical thinking about society and its values (4) Engage in self-reflective thinking about their own life choices; (5) Use writing as a way of further engaging in critical/self-reflective analysis.

The song we analyzed verse-by-verse is the hip-hop rap "I Can" by Nas (2002). He is a fairly well-known rapper for the social and political consciousness often present in his music. Nas criticizes mainstream culture for mis-educating African-American youth while simultaneously reeducating those same youth to understand the greatness in their African heritage and go on to function in and change society. In this song, Nas speaks directly to urban African American youth by encouraging them to make intelligent choices regarding their lives in spite of the many pressures to do wrong. At certain points, he speaks specifically to boys, and then to girls, about the particular difficulties they face. To add to the appeal to young people, Nas uses children to enthusiastically sing the chorus.

I began the lesson by writing the chorus—"I know I can/Be what I want to be/If I work hard at it/I'll be where I want to be"—on the board. However, after I wrote the first four words on the board, several students began singing the song excitedly. Already knowing the answer, I then asked them if those words were familiar to them. Hands immediately shot up. I asked them "Who says these words?" Nearly everyone shouted out "Nas" and others also yelled out the name of the song as well. To initiate an analytical conversation, I questioned the students about what those four lines meant to them. A student named Patrick gave an example: "If you want to be a basketball player, you can't start off dunking. You have to practice hard first."

One young lady, Dianne, responded with "If you do what you know you're supposed to do, it will pay off." "Pay off how?" I asked. Responses varied from "You can get a good job" to "You can get money."

From there we moved to the first four lines of Verse One, which reiterates the chorus:

Be, B-Boys and girls listen up
You can be anything in the world, in God we trust
An architect, doctor, maybe an actress
But nothing comes easy it takes much practice.

The students expressed the understanding that to accomplish something in life, one must be committed to doing what it takes to reach that goal. I asked the students to think about what they want to be when they grow up and what they would have to do in order to reach that goal. One girl said she wants to "deliver babies," and noted that she would have to go to college and to medical school. One young man, who wants to be a dentist, said he knows that he will have to go to college and to "the school to become a dentist." Another young man wanted to be a football player and acknowledged that he will have to "go to college and practice a lot." An additional young lady declared she wants to be a lawyer and that she will attend college and then law school in order to reach her goal. The students clearly had a firm understanding of the song's message and understood that hard work is necessary to meet goals.

After looking at those initial lines of the song, I then played the entire song while the students followed along and read the lyrics, in some cases silently, but in most cases, aloud. In fact, most were rapping along with the song and dancing in their seats. The students were excited and engaged.

Afterwards, we went through the song line by line to perform a close reading. Many students rarely had to look at the lyrics because they were so familiar with the song that they could explain its meaning from memory. They clearly had been paying attention as they listened to this song previously (on the radio) because they very much understood the message—and liked it.

In the second part of Verse Two, Nas tells a story of a young aspiring singer who became associated with the wrong crowd and eventually got involved with drugs:

> Like, I met a woman who's becoming a star
> She was very beautiful leaving people in awe
> Singing songs, Lena Horn, but the younger version
> Hung with the wrong person
> Got her string when I heard . . .
> Sniffing up drugs, all in her nose
> Could have died, so young, now looks ugly and old
> No fun 'cause when she reaches for hugs, people hold they breath
> 'Cause she smells of corrosion and death.

This section sparked great discussion amongst the students. They expressed how people must watch the company they keep so they do not end up in bad situations. They also discussed the negative effects of drugs and laughed as a couple of students cited Whitney Houston as one singer whose beauty and talent have been ruined (allegedly) because of drugs.

The first part of Verse Three is directed specifically toward young girls and the dangers they may face:

> B, B-Boys and girls listen again
> This is for grown-actin' girls who's only ten
> The ones who watch videos and do what they see
> As cute as can be, up in the club with fake IDs
> Careful, 'fore you meet a man with HIV
> You can host the TV like Oprah Winfrey
> Whatever you decide, be careful. Some men
> Be rapists, so act your age, don't pretend to be
> Older than you are, give yourself time to grow
> You thinkin' he can give you wealth, but so?

Again, the students understood the message that young girls should not try to grow up too quickly. Perhaps one girl put it best when she said, with an attitude, "Just because you have the body doesn't mean you grown!" She even got a few "Amens" from classmates who agreed with her statement. Other girls commented on the minimal clothing often worn by girls in videos and giggled and said many "Oooohs" when HIV was mentioned. It appeared that they knew HIV was a "bad" disease, something related to sex, something which they should not necessarily talk about in front of adults. And yet, it was apparent that they understood the message:

> Young boys, you can use a lot of help, you know
> You thinkin' life's all about smokin' . . . and ice
> You don't want to be my age and can't read and write
> Begging different women for a place to sleep at night
> Smart boys turns to men and do whatever they wish
> If you believe you can achieve, then say it like this.

In the second part of Verse Three, we highlighted the line which talks about boys understanding the importance of being responsible, educated, and independent. The dialogue surrounding this verse prompted Patrick to comment on how his mother always tells him, "Your friends will always be there. Outside will always be there. But [the opportunity for] getting good grades will not." Other students noted that if one does not learn to read and write while still young, one may be unable to get a good job or reach the goals one has set.

These comments specifically were of interest to me, especially given the sometimes poor behavior I had observed several days over the course of the school year. So I then asked the students, "If you understand how important an education is to getting a good job and reaching your goals, how come I come in week after week and see people laughing, talking, fooling around, and not turning in work?" I think this point was the most quiet the class had been all year. Before posing this question, I could barely keep the discussion under control because the students were so eager to enter the dialogue. Yet, once I "called them out" (as the children would say), or directly made the students aware of their responsibilities, they were quiet.

Again, I posed the question, asking why they were suddenly so quiet. After a few moments, students slowly began to respond to the question. Patrick and Roi talked about how they get distracted when they see their friends playing and not doing their work. Others complained of being tired. Still, others complained of having "too much homework." Interestingly, though, Brielle, "checked" her peers on that issue by saying, "You only got all that homework because you don't follow directions in class."

I then decided to pose the same question (regarding the lack of seriousness and responsibility where school is concerned) in the context of the students' African ancestry. We quickly turned to Verse Three:

> Be, before we came to this country
> We were kings and queens, never porch monkeys
> There was empires in Africa called Kush
> Timbuktu, where every race came to get books
> To learn from Black teachers who taught Greeks and Romans
> Asians, Arabs, and gave them gold when
> Gold was converted to money it all changed
> Money then became empowerment for Europeans.

In this third verse, Nas clearly is telling the history of African civilizations with key examples of the knowledge and inventions people of these empires created. The students commented on how many people do not give respect to or acknowledge Africans and their great contributions. We then moved on:

> The Persian military invaded
> They heard about the gold, the teachings, and everything sacred
> Africa was almost robbed naked
> Slavery was money, so they began making slave ships
> Egypt was the place that Alexander the Great went
> He was so shocked that the mountains has faces
> Shot up they nose to impose what basically
> Still goes on today, you see?

This part of Verse Three prompted students to discuss the ills of slavery. Some students commented on the harsh conditions slaves endured—very little food, water, or shelter, not to mention their families often being torn apart and their inability to learn to read and write. So again, I turned the discussion back to the students by saying, "People fought and died for you to be here, to be free and able to get an education. So why don't you take it seriously when our ancestors fought so hard?" The students, again, were quiet; then, a few discussed how people now take their education for granted. In a connected thought, Jessia remembered a history lesson about Blacks being worth only 3/5 a White man and that they did not have the right to vote. She commented that she knows several adults who do not vote, and she could not understand why.

They went on to question numerous issues affecting the Black community, one of them being why there are so many Blacks in jail. A few students answered this question by saying some people are just ignorant. Others delved deeper by saying that many African Americans have had hard lives and had to resort to stealing for survival. Patrick noted that sometimes people are just in the wrong place at the wrong time. He went on to cite the example that one person may steal something, and then the friend may "go down" with him because of their association. We, as a class, then took that example and related it back to Verse One, in which Nas tells youngsters to watch the company they keep for fear of bringing trouble to themselves.

Perhaps the last verse of Nas's song best summarizes his message to African-American youth:

> If the truth is told, the youth can grow
> They learn to survive until they gain control
> Nobody says you have to be gangsters
> Read more, learn more, change the globe
> Ghetto children, do your thing
> Hold you head up little man, you're a king
> Young princess when you get your wedding ring
> Your man will sing "She's my queen."

The first two lines of this verse, in effect, echo Carter G. Woodson's notion that true growth and success can only come when African Americans are accurately educated about the history of America and themselves. In his text *The Mis-Education of the Negro*, Woodson (1990/1933) argues that most "educated" African Americans have not been educated at all, for what they have learned is a distorted view of the world that ignores the contributions that Blacks have made. He then argues that African Americans have been "mis-educated" and must reeducate themselves first to be aware and then to have pride in the history of their ancestors. Nas's song serves as one way of fulfilling Woodson's goal, for it not only tells a brief history of Africans and the devastating effects of slavery, but also of the great accomplishments of African civilizations. Nas encourages children to realize their worth as descendants of African kings and queens so they can educate themselves and ultimately change the world.

THE STUDENTS' WRITTEN RESPONSES:
WHAT ARE THEY REALLY SAYING?

I finally calmed the students down enough to ask them to write a paragraph about what this song meant to them and how they will live their lives in order to reach their goals. In other words, I used the class discussion as a collaborative brainstorming session. What I expected to occur and what actually happened varied greatly. It was not the content of their responses that surprised me, but rather the form in which they were written. Although the students had communicated verbally in some variation of the Black Dialect, their paragraphs were written primarily in Standard English. Though there were some students who indeed did construct some sentences in Black Dialect, overall, even with the grammatical errors that several students made, it was obvious that their intent was to write in Standard English. One student, Jessia, focused on the last verse of the song:

> . . . It says if the truth is told than youth can grow. I think that verse means you should never live through a lie. Or you should not live on what you think happened, you should live on the truth and nothing but the truth.

She was drawn to the last verse perhaps because she understood that for many young African Americans the truth of their history has been hidden. These sentences, along with her comments during class, make clear that she comprehends Nas's message.

The majority of the responses, however, were centered on the idea that these youth could reach their goals if they worked hard, made smart choices about their lives, and believed in themselves:

> The song is basically about achieving what you want to do without smoking drugs doing what you see, acting older than you are, in the club with fake ID. (Auraina)

> These lines mean that we can be anything that we want to be. If we work hard at it. If we go to school we can become these things. I want to be a lawyer and got to go to law school. (Jarrel)

> To me this song means that children can be whatever they want to (as far as careers) when they grow up, only if they try and do what they're supposed to. The goals I want to be are to go to Harvard Medical School, and become an obstetrician. (Amarrah)

These messages exemplify the students' belief that the world is full of great possibilities for themselves if they have the self-confidence and commitment to work hard and stay focused on their goals. The student responses also demonstrate, as Bakari Kitwana (2002) notes in his text *The Hip Hop Generation*, that many young African Americans do believe they are entitled to a piece of the American Dream and that it should be obtainable because of the struggles of their ancestors.

Thus, the duality of identity continues to be apparent, but we do see evidence of students working to intertwine the two selves. During our in-class lesson, students used Black Dialect to cite the ills of slavery and question certain societal conditions. Yet when it came to their written responses, they showed a desire to be accepted into mainstream society by their use of Standard English (just as Nas uses a mixture of Black Dialect and Standard English) and their desire to obtain mainstream success.

Nas's words were effective in helping the students achieve all of the objectives for this lesson. Through our in-class discussion, the students performed a close reading; communicated their feelings about the song's message; questioned current societal conditions; considered the implications of their own life choices; and, through their writing, they continued that self-reflection and analysis of their lives.

Had we more time, I would have liked to have turned this writing assignment into a formal one where we focused on creating solid thesis statements with strong supporting sentences to follow, and then paid attention to organization, grammar, and mechanics. Because of the nature of the content, I would make this into a collaborative writing assignment where the class discussion would serve as a brainstorming session. Then, I would separate the students into groups of three or four, being sure to include stronger and weaker writers in each group. As a group, the students would have to create on paragraph explaining the overall message of the song. Next, each student would write his or her own paragraph detailing his or her goals in life and the attitudes and actions required to reach them. Lastly, the group would create one document for their African-American peers explaining what steps they can do to be successful in life, why those steps are important, and why being successful is essential to themselves as individuals, to the African-American community, and to our country. This group assignment may be one that would extend over the course of several days; however, the benefits would be worth it, for the students would experience the various stages of the writing process in order to create a document that would really matter to them.

Unfortunately, I was allowed only one class session with the students. Yet, just in about one hour, I saw students who were previously inattentive and disinterested, become actively engaged, excited about course content that included them, and willing to think and write critically.

Though this lesson does not reach its full potential, the implications are worth noting. The students' willingness to actively participate suggests that, as Ladson-Billings' theory claims, students will be more comfortable with pursuing excellence in the classroom when they are allowed to establish and maintain a positive racial identity. As for writing, the students' desire to write in Standard English (when they primarily spoke the African American Vernacular) is worth noting.

In his text *Let's Flip the Script: An African American Discourse on Language, Literature, and Learning*, Keith Gilyard (1996) identifies three camps with which Compositionists may choose to associate. The first group of theorists, eradicationists, says that schools should destroy Black English because it represents deficient speech and interferes with the acquisition of Standard English. The second camp, bidialecticalists, takes an accomodationist attitude. They argue that Black English speakers need Standard English to succeed in mainstream society, but they do not embrace the function and value of Black English for its speakers. The third group of educators, of which Gilyard is a proponent, is the pluralist camp. These teachers believe that while students should be prepared for the real world, Black English should not be treated so negatively in the classroom. They understand that most of the educational problems encountered by speakers of Black English stem not from the dialect they use, but from who they are as people. Thus, these instructors fight to get Black English some "real respect," while not ignoring that in a more equitable learning environment, students generally would want to learn Standard English and how to make it their own language (p. 70). The key, then, to the pluralist ideology is that if the experiences, particularly the literacy practices, of students are respected and embraced *first*, then students are more willing to learn in the writing classroom.

The students' active participation and collaboration with the Nas exercise illustrates Gilyard's claim. The affective component of instruction, specifically writing instruction, is more powerful than many secondary teachers realize. We, as teachers, must be persistent and diligent in creating more assignments such as the one described here. Students of color need to know that their experiences matter in the classroom and connect them to the larger society. We should not force students to choose one self over another. They should be allowed to be their full selves—the selves that love African American culture and the selves that strive to receive straight A's—in our writing classrooms at all times.

REFERENCES

Baldwin, J. (1998). If Black English isn't a language, then tell me, what is? In T. Perry & L. Delpit (Eds.) *The real Ebonics debate: Power, language, and the education of African-American children.* (pp. 67–76). Boston: Beacon Press. (Original work published 1979)

Ball, A., & Lardner, T. (1997). Dispositions toward a language: Teacher constructs of knowledge and the Ann Arbor Black English case. *College Composition and Communication,* 48(4), 469–85.

Gilyard, K. (1991). *Voices of the self: A study of language competence.* Detroit, MI: Wayne State University Press.

Gilyard, K. (1996). *Let's flip the script: Discourse on language and literacy learning.* Detroit, MI: Wayne State University Press.

Kitwana, B. (2002). *The hip hop generation: young blacks and the crisis in African-American culture.* New York: Basic Books.

Ladson-Billings, G. (1994). *The dreamkeepers: Successful teachers of African American children.* San Francisco: Jossey-Bass Publishing.

Nas. (2002). I know I can. On *God's Son.* [CD]. New York: Sony/BMG Records.

Smitherman, G. (1977). *Talkin' and testifying: The language of Black America.* Detroit: Wayne State University Press.

Villanueva, V. (1993). *Bootstraps: From an American academic of color.* Urbana, IL: National Council of Teachers of English.

Woodson, C.G. (1990). *The miseducation of the Negro.* Trenton, NJ: Africa World Press. (Original work published 1933)

CHAPTER 9

THE POWER OF THEIR TEXTS

Using Hip Hop to Help Urban Students Meet NCTE/IRA National Standards for the English Language Arts

David E. Kirkland

ABSTRACT

While goals for English language arts are expanding, curriculum and instruction within English language arts classrooms remain exclusionary. As such, marginalized urban youth struggle to meet national standards for reading comprehension and writing. To address this dilemma, I discuss ways in which Hip Hop might be used to include marginalized students and help promote proficiency in writing.

According to the NCTE/IRA Standards for the English Language Arts:

- Students will read a wide range of print and non-print texts *to build an understanding of texts, of themselves, and of the cultures of the United States and the world*; to acquire new information; to respond to the needs and demands of society and the workplace; and for personal fulfillment. Among these texts are fiction and nonfiction, classic and *contemporary* works.

Closing the Gap, pages 129–145

- Students will *apply a wide range of strategies to comprehend, interpret, evaluate, and appreciate texts. They draw on their prior experience, their interactions with other readers and writers, their knowledge of word meaning and of other texts,* their word identification strategies, and their understanding of textual features (e.g., sound-letter correspondence, sentence structure, context, graphics).

- Students employ *a wide range of strategies as they write and use different writing process elements* appropriately to *communicate with different audiences* for a variety of purposes.

- Students apply knowledge of language structure, language conventions (e.g., spelling and punctuation), media techniques, figurative language, and genre *to create, critique, and discuss print and nonprint texts.* (1996, p. 1; emphasis added)

Since NCTE/IRA produced their national standards in 1996, curriculum and instruction in secondary English settings have shifted. Many English language arts classrooms began to offer students a broad range of textual choices, somewhat reflecting the diversity of American society. In spite of this shift, texts authored by White males still dominate English language arts classrooms. As such, urban students—many of whom are not White—rarely study or write about texts in their English language arts classrooms that reflect their interests and cultural heritage. As a result, many urban students feel alienated within schools (Mahiri, 1998) and, worse, struggle to meet national reading and writing standards.

This paper deals, specifically, with this disconnection between urban students and the NCTE/IRA English language arts writing standards. In order to reach these students and help them attain the writing standards set for them, I argue that Hip Hop, which Smitherman (1999, p. 269) calls the "voice of urban America," is ideal for the production of a culturally relevant English pedagogy capable of engaging urban students in sustained and critical English study.

HIP HOP AS TEXTS

There are ongoing debates in English education concerning what constitutes a text. The perspective on text that guides this paper is drawn from poststructural theories. Derrida (1976, 1982) counts text as anything that is articulated, thus suggesting that text can be much more than print on a page. In this way, Wade and Moje (2000) contend,

Texts, then, are organized networks that people generate or use to make meaning either for themselves or for others. Texts can be formalized and permanent, reproduced as books or speeches and sold as commodities. Or, they can be informal and fleeting—written lists or notes that are scribbled out and quickly thrown away, or conversations and performances that are made permanent only as they are written or recorded by sound or video devices or passed on orally to other people. . . . Different views of what counts as text—whether they are formal and informal; oral, written, enacted; permanent or fleeting—lead to different views of what counts as learning, and consequently expand or limit the opportunities students have to learn in classrooms. (p. 610)

Student learning in the secondary English classrooms (as the NCTE/IRA standards suggest) consists of student engagement with texts. However, as Morrell and Duncan-Andrade (2002) point out, many urban students fail to engage (read or write about) traditional classroom texts, either because such texts lack relevance to them (Ladson-Billings, 1996) or because such texts promote perspectives and interests that are threatening to them. By limiting our understanding of texts to traditional, canonical literature, we limit the opportunities urban students have to write in our English classrooms.

By saying this, I am not saying that urban students do not engage with texts. They are, in fact, engrossed in textual practices. As one student told me, "I am a Hip Hop head," which spoke not only of his interest in Hip Hop as music, but in his knowledge of Hip Hop as texts. To him, Hip Hop was something to know. In addition to being able to read it, he was in constant dialogue with it—writing it, writing about it, and writing through it. Hence, I use Hip Hop to refer to something more than music. In this way, I refer to Hip Hop as the post-revolutionary, urban movement which responded to the passing of civil rights and Black power and the failure of industrialism. Urban youth in the Bronx, New York, fermented the Hip Hop movement as a way to voice their criticism of racism, neglect, and economic oppression in urban Black America. Powell (1991) describes Hip Hop this way:

[Hip Hop/Rap] emerged from the streets of inner-city neighborhoods as a genuine reflection of the hopes, concerns, and aspirations of urban Black youth in this, the last quarter of the 20th century. Rap is essentially a homemade, street-level musical genre . . . Rap lyrics concentrate primarily on the contemporary African American experience. . . . Every issue within the Black community is subject to exposition in the rap arena. Hit rap tunes have broached touchy subjects such as sex, sexism, racism, and crime. (p. 25)

In addition to being a "musical genre," Hip Hop represents an artistic shift in American society reminiscent of the Harlem Renaissance of the 1920s. As both culture and art, "Hip Hop is manifested in such cultural productions as graffiti art, break dancing, styles of dress (e.g., baggy pants, sneakers, Malcolm X caps, appropriately worn backward), love of b-ball (basketball), and so forth" (Smitherman, 1999, p. 268). Urban youth, through Hip Hop, developed radical new cultural dance practices like crip walkin (exported from the West Coast), new ways of resistance writing like taggin and tattooing, and innovative linguistic expressions such as "phat" (spelled with *ph* to indicate high quality or excellence).

Most important, Hip Hop is text. According to Smitherman (1999), "[Hip Hop] is not only a Black expressive cultural phenomenon; it is, at the same time, a resisting discourse, a set of communicative practices that constitute a *text* of resistance..." (p. 270; emphasis added). Adding to Smitherman's idea, Morrell and Duncan-Andrade (2002) "argue that Hip-hop texts are literary texts and can be used to scaffold literary terms and concepts and ultimately foster literary interpretations" (p. 89). As such, Hip Hop texts can be used to promote writing and critical classroom dialogue among urban students around serious social issues pertaining to resistance and struggle, race and gender, and cultural exploitation. In the English classroom, this dialogue, while transactive, can be transformative. Not only can it foster student engagement, but it can also stimulate movement among a growing number of urban students who are, by default, being left behind.

While it might be helpful in closing "the achievement gap," teaching Hip Hop in secondary English classrooms serves a greater good. It can be useful in integrating a culturally homogeneous curriculum that has, for the decades since *Brown V. Board of Education*, been resistant to change. That is, Hip Hop presents itself as a fresh, new text that deals with the diversity and complexities of postmodern America (Kirkland, 2006). This freshness makes Hip Hop relevant to many urban students, who also deal with the complexities and diversities of urban life.

Because of what they share, Hip Hop and urban students can be brought together in pedagogical allegiance to stimulate transformative discussions, actively engaged citizenship, and a critical writing practice (Kirkland, 2005). As such, Hip Hop can be used to help students, particularly urban students, develop the critical competencies needed to legislate social change and spark empowerment in their communities. In addition to using it to stimulate action, Hip Hop can also prompt critical reflection. That is, urban students can analyze (reflect upon and write about) Hip Hop (in relation to their lives or other analytical constructs) to acquire the dispositions needed to comprehend, interpret, evaluate, and appreciate texts.

With this in mind, we must not, however, lose site of students' existing relationships with familiar texts, especially Hip Hop. As Brown (2005) points out, not all urban students are interested in Hip Hop the same way.

In addition, teachers who are unprepared to use Hip Hop in the classroom may not be able to effectively engage students in either discussion or analysis of texts related to the genre. Hence, it is important that English teachers who use Hip Hop in the classroom understand two basic issues that could influence student writing:

- Relevance (some students do not explicitly relate to Hip Hop just as some students do not explicitly relate to Shakespeare).
- Teacher Preparation (just as teaching Shakespeare requires sustained study and planning on the part of the teacher, so does teaching Hip Hop).

While it may help engage some students, teaching Hip Hop does not guarantee an engaged classroom.

In addition to these two pedagogical issues, there is another matter that deserves some attention. Hip Hop struggles with "real," complex, provocative, and sometimes controversial issues. With this in mind, Richardson (2003) warns, "The music and lyrics [of Hip Hop] must be considered in relation to beliefs, values, mores, and complex ideologies that underlie the street apparel, hard body imagery, and the sometimes seeming celebration of misogyny, thuggishness, and larger than life personas narrated in the music" (p. 69). But much of what is critiqued in Hip Hop is not Hip Hop's alone.

Many Hip Hop texts are explicit about America's culture of violence, misogyny, and greed. In this way, Richardson (2003) argues, "The weight American society places on the acquisition of wealth and material possessions, patriarchy and the social construction of maleness as a means of power and prestige are also factors in the production of the music, lyrics, expressive behaviors and its focus on materiality, sex, and power by many [Hip Hop] artists" (p. 70). While they are present in Hip Hop, the "American cultural themes" of materiality, sex, and power are, as well, eminent in canonical texts that have been used to teach English for decades. Teachers who claim they cannot "teach" Hip Hop because of such issues or because of Hip Hop's so-called "inappropriateness" raise disturbing questions about the enduring remnants of institutional racism and curricular segregation in K–12 classroom settings.

A final pedagogical issue that must be addressed deals with Hip Hop as a fad. In her critique of Hip Hop's educational popularity, Brown (2005) described the misguided celebration and exploitation of Hip Hop in the classroom. She maintains that Hip Hop can be tokenized by teachers, who fail to explore critical issues that, if ignored, perpetuate ignorance and injustice. By glossing over important issues within the genre, teaching Hip Hop will be as effective as watching "the movie to the book on Friday." While simply watching the movie might entertain them, students will not gain much from uncritical encounters with texts (Morrell, 2004). Hence, in order to prevent tokenizing it, we must have students seriously engage Hip Hop, in ways that push them to make sense of it and the world around them.

TEACHING HIP HOP IN THE SECONDARY ENGLISH CLASSROOM

Recent national achievement data illustrate a literacy gap among America's urban and non-urban youth. While we have very good evidence to conclude that urban youth are engaged in sophisticated textual practices (Appleman, 2000; Dyson, 2003; Fisher, 2003; Morrell, 2004), opportunities for this kind of textual engagement are rarely presented in English classrooms. Morrell and Duncan-Andrade (2002) note that urban youth, through Hip Hop, exhibit "the critical and analytical skills that we want them to bring to academic texts from the canon" (p. 88). In this way, Richardson (2003), in her study of African American literacies, found that [Black] students possess a variety of (critical) "literacies and consciousnesses" that come out of Hip Hop. Richardson (2003), further, notes, when they have official opportunities to engage in the critical study of Hip Hop, students' performances on official literacy tasks, like academic writing, improve dramatically (Richardson, 2003, pp. 68–72).

While there is evidence that Hip Hop can be used to help students meet learning objectives, questions persist. Specifically, there is little information on (1) how to use Hip Hop to most effectively teach students to write and, thereby, deal with complexities and dilemmas of texts; (2) how to use Hip Hop to teach language, especially in light of the primacy of standard English in our schools and society; and (3) how (and if) teaching Hip Hop can be used to prepare students for standardized assessments, college admissions, and the world of work. While it is important for students to engage relevant texts in classrooms, it is equally important for students to learn academic literacies, which are the standardized uses of language and texts in American society. Given this dilemma, we have to continue to consider how teaching Hip Hop can be used to meet national English language arts standards.

The rest of this paper will address two questions related to the concerns stated above:

- How can teachers use Hip Hop to help urban students meet national standards for the English Language Arts (in particular, the NCTE/ IRA writing standards)?
- How can teachers use Hip Hop to help urban students exceed national (writing) standards?

THE CCW UNIT

In order to answer these questions, I designed a unit (the CCW unit) that two Michigan State University intern teachers, whom I supervised, used in their classrooms. The unit deals with various theories of Hip Hop (Kitwana, 2003; Morgan, 1999; Pough, 2004), specifically theories related to the unit's theme, "The Classroom, the Community, and the World." In this way, we approached Hip Hop as a Black cultural aesthetic, which commented on human experience from an Afro-urban perspective.

The conceptualization of the CCW unit was not confined to Hip Hop theories alone. The unit employed other critical literacy frames, which Appleman (2000) maintains "can help secondary literature classrooms become sites of constructive and transactive activity where students approach texts with curiosity, authority, and initiative" (p. 9). In particular, the unit employed three approaches to literature that Appleman outlines: Rosenblatt's (1968) reader-response, feminist literary theory (Showalter, 1989), and Marxist literary theory (Appleman, 2000). In bringing these perspectives to bear on Hip Hop text, students composed texts that dealt with multiple aspects of our humanity. Specifically, they were able to build understandings of the texts, of themselves, and of others. Not only did the critical analytical lenses make visible what our students brought to the texts, but it also gave them language to articulate this interaction, rooted in cultural and social critique.

Hip Hop texts were far more amenable than canonical texts to critical analysis, perhaps because they emanate from textual genres rooted in critique of contemporary circumstances. Along these lines, Morrell and Duncan-Andrade (2002) contend,

> Teaching Hip-hop as a music and culture of resistance can facilitate the development of critical consciousness in urban youth. Analyzing the critical social commentary produced by [Hip Hop] may lead to consciousness-raising discussions, essays, and research projects attempting to locate an explanation for the current state of affairs for urban youngsters. The knowledge reflected in these lyrics could engender discussions of esteem, power, place, and purpose or encourage students to further their own knowledge of urban sociology and politics. In this way, Hip hop music should stand on its own merit in the academy and be a worthy subject of study in its own right rather than necessarily leading to something more "acceptable" like a Shakespearean [sic] text. (pp. 89–90)

M. A. K. Halliday's (1980) "three aspects of language study" also helped to shape the CCW unit. According to Halliday (1980), a child learns language, through language and about language. Hence, the process of learning is as much about learning context as it is about learning content. Then, to teach Hip Hop content divorced from the context to which it belongs diminishes its educational value. In this way, the CCW unit required students to learn Hip Hop by reading lyrics and listening to music from several artists. Texts ranged from Run DMC's "Walk This Way" to NWA's "Expression," from "Queen Latifah's "U-N-I-T-Y," to Lil' Kim's "Heavenly Father." Students also wrote raps, some of which were thematic and others more open ended.

LEARNING HIP HOP

While they were exposed to several Hip Hop texts, students closely examined two songs ("Dear Momma" and "Changes") by posthumous rap artist Tupac Shakur. These texts were looked at closely to answer the question: what is Hip Hop? To answer the question, students looked at the Hip Hop texts to determine what was happening in the texts (e.g., What was the function of words and phrases? How was meaning and experience expressed?). For example, students identified a list of literary concepts ranging from metaphor to alliteration and from chiasmus to irony. As they analyzed the texts, students used their knowledge of such terms to assess each rap's literary merit. Building upon this activity, students developed their own "rules for writing rap" and used these "rules" to compose their own raps.

Student raps varied in style and in substance. In spite of their differences, all of the student-produced raps emanated from known Hip Hop traditions. Some of the student-produced raps were overtly political like the raps of KRS-1, Public Enemy, and Mos Def. Other student-produced raps were comical like the raps of DJ Jazzy Jeff and the Fresh Prince and, more recently, Kanye West. Still others were a sober reflection of city-street life, reminiscent of the raps of N.W.A., Notorious B.I.G., and the Game. The objective, here, was not to use rap to scaffold academic literacy (basic writing) skills. Rather, the objective was to have students learn Hip Hop by having them practice it. Listening to, reading, and writing raps was our way of accomplishing this goal.

Learning about Hip Hop

The CCW unit also promoted students' learning about Hip Hop—its history, its language, and its culture—by exposing students to a wide range of texts that provide information on what Hip Hop is about. To learn about Hip Hop's language, students read Smitherman's (1997) "The Chain Remain the Same: Communicative Practices in the Hip Hop Nation" (pp.

268–283). Our objective was not to dismiss the importance of learning Standard English, but rather to present material that might help students appreciate their own languages. According to Smitherman (1999), "It is critical to keep in mind that the racialized rhetoric of rap music and the Hip Hop Nation is embodied in the communicative practices of the larger Black speech community" (p. 271). Hence, the language of Hip Hop has deep roots, especially for urban students, many of whom are Black. Since Black language has been devalued and vilified in our society, it was important for us to establish the legitimacy of Black language in Hip Hop so that students would not feel that they were reading "inferior" texts.

In addition to language study, students read excerpts from Light's (1999) *Vibe Magazine's History of Hip Hop* and Kitwanna's (2003) *The Hip Hop Nation*. These texts were used to help students explore Hip Hop's evolution over time and to help introduce them to the cultural study of Hip Hop. In this way, students learned that, just as it has legitimate linguistic roots, Hip Hop also has legitimate historical and cultural roots. By exploring the deeper characteristics of Hip Hop, students gained valuable contextual knowledge about the Hip Hop texts they were reading and writing about. This knowledge was crucial in helping reform students' understanding of themselves, which was vital to getting them to write about texts in more sophisticated and valued ways. As such, students began to understand how they could learn through Hip Hop about the world. Hence, as they learned about it, students began to associate Hip Hop with other valued products that they consumed, appreciated, and critiqued.

Learning Through Hip Hop

Finally, the CCW unit encouraged students to learn through Hip Hop. In the course of the unit, we explored, analyzed, and evaluated many themes related to human experience. In this way, students developed understandings and interpretations of the many dimensions of human experience and developed an awareness of how texts, including Hip Hop texts, speak to one another and to various conditions that define individuals and the world. Some students commented on the Black mother/son relationship, comparing Tupac's "Dear Momma" and Hughes's "Mother to Son." Other students explored femininity, deconstructing beauty in Walker's "Everyday Use," TLC's "Unpretty," and Aguilera's "Beautiful." In this way, Hip Hop was used to sanction ideas that relate to much more than Hip Hop. Specifically, our students were learning how to critically analyze texts, through which they could make sense of the world.

Meeting the Standards ... and More

During the course of the CCW unit, students produced texts that demonstrated their proficiency with respect to NCTE/IRA writing standards. Not only did students read a wide-range of texts, but they were also able to demonstrate an understanding of these texts in writing. They were also able to "apply knowledge of language structure, language conventions (e.g., spelling and punctuation), media techniques, figurative language, and genre to *create, critique, and discuss* [these] print and nonprint texts" (emphasis added).

The following episode illustrates this point:

> **S:** I can relate to what Tupac feels in his rap 'Dear Momma.' It come[s] from the same place that make[s] Hughes write his poem—the heart. This is where we all share a universal love for momma. She [is] the same to all of us. She [is] momma. No matter where she is, who[se mother] she is, she got [has] the same name: Momma.
>
> **T:** But Hughes does not call the mother in his poem Momma.
>
> **S:** They [are] still alike ... (stutters), re-related. Hughes's poem [has] a mother talking to her son, you know, giving him some advice. [Tu]Pac is a son, saying thank you for what his mother [has given] him. Don't Hughes got a poem called "Thank you" too?
>
> **T:** That's a short story, "Thank you, Ma'am." Go on.
>
> **S:** I don't know ... (Pauses) Whether your momma is like Langton Hughes's mother or like Tupac's momma, she [is] a symbol of love to us all.

What is distinctive about this episode is that the student is making observations about a perceived relationship that he believes exists between two unlike texts which share commonalities. Even when challenged by his teacher, the student maintains: "They still alike." His insistence that his interpretation of the texts (that the mother figure in Black writing is a powerful character) is valid and telling. Much scholarly writing is about authority in making truth claims, supporting/establishing a rationale for such claims, and labeling what is perceived in the world. Hence, the episode takes on scholarly characteristics. It suggests that the student has become able to identify relationships in texts and make those relationships real, support their reality, defend them, and label them (e.g., "She got the same name: Momma").

Further, the texts did not serve as a source of information for the student. To use the terminology of Rosenblatt: his is not an "efferent" read. Rather, the student in this particular episode uses the texts as a tool for thinking about and examining the Black mother/son relationship. According to Wade and Moje (2000), these kinds of connections and interpretations of texts constitute engagement. According to the NCTE/IRA Standards for the English Language Arts (1996), this student's engagement represents learning. As I will demonstrate, this learning—while evident in this discussion—is also evident in students' writings.

In the course of the CCW unit, students completed a culminating writing assignment. The assignment asked students to respond to a theme in their readings and analyze Hip Hop in some personal way. Both the structure and the language of the writing assignment were consistent with the language of the Michigan Education Assessment Program (MEAP) writing test (Michigan Department of Education, 2003). In her final essay, a student offered an interpretation of the mother/son theme (the same theme discussed above) in the texts "Mother to Son" and "Dear Momma." Her written response demonstrates high-level writing proficiency with respect to the NCTE/IRA national standards. According to the student,

> The symbol of the mother in both of the texts ["Mother to Son" and "Dear Momma"] has a lot of importance for how we think of women today. There is a hidden tension: she is a savior and a survivor... but a sinner and a saint. Women in our society have usually been boxed up between paradoxical extremes, which never allow us to see who she really might be—always more than what we think she is—more than a friend, more than just a mother, but, like Lil' Kim said—a woman, a phenomenal woman.

In her analysis of the "woman character" in the two texts, the student feels put off by the male (or "mother to son") depiction of the mother. For her, this description, while celebratory, is restricting. Her assessment is similar to the feminist literary criticism of hooks (1992) and others, who find it limiting to describe women in extreme terms, "as sinner or saint," as Mammy or Jezebel. As such, there is sophisticated analysis taking place in the brief excerpt, which indicates learning and proficiency.

According to the NCTE/IRA writing standards, "students [will] employ *a wide range of strategies as they write and use different writing process elements* appropriately to *communicate with different audiences* for a variety of purposes." Indeed, this student has employed a feminist strategy to write about the mother character in "Mother to Son" and "Dear Momma" in a very sophisticated way. The standards also indicate that "students [will] apply knowledge of language structure, language conventions (e.g., spelling and punctuation), media techniques, figurative language, and genre *to create, critique, and discuss print and non-print texts.*" While written in standard

English, there is certainly an awareness of language (i.e., what it means to be a mother) that pervades the text. As such, her writing employs a variety of complex language structures.

In the example given, the student blends a poetic voice ("always more than what we think she is—more than a friend, more than just a mother") with a salient argument ("women in our society have usually been boxed up between paradoxical extremes"). While I have only established that this student's writing meets national standards, it also suggests that the serious study of Hip Hop can be an avenue to encourage student writing.

What I have done thus far is illustrate that Hip Hop in collaboration with other textual material can, in fact, be used for serious study in English language arts. That is, students can write compellingly about Hip Hop and Hip Hop texts. Not only can it stimulate complex and sophisticated discussion and analysis, but it can also invite prolific written responses that live up to, and in many cases exceed, national writing standards. But what else can Hip Hop in secondary English education offer? In short, it can offer a lot.

With the achievement gap in literacy looming large, it is urgent that English educators revise instruction in ways that engage disengaged and marginalized urban students. This means shifting our focus away from a narrow curriculum designed around the English canon and substituting texts with which disengaged urban students are most familiar (i.e., Hip Hop texts). While the examples above illustrate ways that students can discuss and write about Hip Hop in a serious and thoughtful manner, they also hint at what Hip Hop means to urban students. Indeed, it is very much a source of contention, conversation, celebration, and critique.

Another student, described by my interns as "disengaged," "failing," "not-working," in fact, successfully engaged with the CCW unit. The student described the unit as "real," commenting on "the things we listen to" outside of the classroom as relevant for the classroom. While it may be a moot point, during the CCW unit, the student did not miss a day of class. During that time, I asked him how he felt about the unit:

> **Student:** It's a good unit. I like it [pause] 'cause the stuff we talking about is real. I'm saying, it's not like the other stuff we was doing. I'm talking about reading stuff that don't make sense, listening to the teachers talk in big words about stuff we read that don't make no sense, and then, we got to write about it. I can't do that.
>
> **Me:** Can't do what.
>
> **S:** Write about stuff that don't make no sense. All I can say is it don't make no sense, or it's boring.
>
> **Me:** What about now?

S: I like what we doing now 'cause I like rap and Hip Hop. Sometimes that way they talk about [Hip Hop] and teach it is boring, but it is usually real interesting, like the conversation we had the other day about drugs killing Black people. I can git wit that. [stutters] I can relate. I see drugs killing Black people every day. I can't relate to Shakespeare. I don't see brothas climbing into sistas windows saying wack stuff like 'wherefore art thou' boo. That's just not real to me.

The same student in his writing assignment analyzed Hip Hop, constructing a well-thought out argument. In his final paper, this student compared the origins of Hip Hop to its current state. According to the student,

> You can think [about] hip hop in two ways: the hip hop of yesterday and the hip hop of today. Both hip hops have significance but unfortunately they do not mean the same. The hip hop of yesterday was originally based on cultural relationships, resistance to dominant cultural and social forms, creative expression, and stories from people's everyday lives. Its popularity was based on its relationship to the poor and disadvantage black community, which was a rejection of other forms of black music commodified by white corporate America. Hip hop today is, in fact, a major part of the white American corporate machine. Today's hip hop is based on the exotic: the minstrel show of modern America where black people's lives are put on stage and exploited for the benefit of the corporate enterprise.

Not only does this student's written response deal with change over time, but it also deals with the politics of economic power and influence. Indeed, reading other texts in conjunction with Hip Hop texts (and with the help of teachers and multiple revisions), this student was able to produce/compose a complex analytic piece of writing. In this way, the student demonstrates knowledge of a range of ideas (e.g., a Hip Hop of today and a Hip Hop of yesterday) and textual approaches (i.e., Appleman's [2000] Marxist approach). While this student's critique of Hip Hop employs elements of Marxist literary interpretation, I argue that Marx did not make Hip Hop visible to the student, but the other way around—Hip Hop has made Marx (and other complex approaches to literature) visible to the student.

After his final paper was written, I spoke with the student again:

Me: Do you like to write?

S: I think that question is unfair. I write sometime, but I don't like to write in here. I write at home sometimes. But in school, we usually don't get to write about stuff like this [Hip Hop]

Me: I'm sorry. Maybe I should ask, how was this experience for you?

S: Good . . . I guess. You mean my paper.

Me: Yeah, let's talk about your paper.

S: I like my paper. My teachers say they like it. It's the only paper I finished this year. I guess it show that I can do it [write proficiently] when I want to. I mean, I ain't no dummy.

Me: No . . . we know that. But why aren't you showing us all the time what you are capable of?

S: That's a hard question. [Pause] I don't be thinking that school is, like, the place for me, not because I can't do the work. I be doing it, and all I can think about is what the . . . what does this have to do with me. I don't be seeing my moms reading stuff like the stuff we read in here or nobody else outside school. It's, like, school is so detached from my reality. I know I don't fit in here, and they don't do much to help.

Me: But, as you admitted, you wrote a great paper.

S: That's 'cause it was about Hip Hop. We talk about that stuff on the street. Me and friends always argue about Hip Hop and stuff like that. There is even movies like *Brown Sugar* talking Hip Hop today versus Hip Hop yesterday. I can write about Hip Hop because I talk about it all the time.

This brief transcript of conversation suggests that the student felt enabled by the presence of and opportunity to write about Hip Hop in his classroom. Hence, by inviting Hip Hop into the classroom, we also invited this student (his world and his experiences) into the classroom as well. So what Hip hop has to offer, especially to historically left-out groups like many of our urban youth, is an invitation. In some ways and for some students, it promises to make the study of English more real and the practice of writing more authentic. Students who feel ostracized in English classrooms might feel more accepted when we embrace Hip Hop in pedagogy. Furthermore, students who are not currently meeting standards might become encouraged to learn once they feel accepted and connected to their learning.

CONCLUSION

Taken together, the writing examples and conversational episodes mentioned above describe the meanings that students are capable of making when given an opportunity to seriously engage their texts. In *The Reader, the Text, and the Poem*, Rosenblatt (1978) argues for a transactional view of literary response. This view holds that literature demands a particular kind of attention in which the reader's experience is as important as the text being read. The transaction between text and reader's experience (as text) becomes a third text, or the poem. The poem represents the potential of responses (written and otherwise) that can be articulated when a reader makes a connection with a text. Yet, as suggested above, it is difficult for students to connect with texts in which they find little relevance.

As I alluded to earlier, the issue of engaging disengaged students really is not about literary approach. Texts become meaningful for various reasons and, indeed, we derive meaning from texts based upon the connections that we share with them. The issue here, then, is about the relationship, the explicit connection, between the reader and the text. Divorced of this connection a text can render little meaning to a reader/writer. Hence, the interpretations that the students produced (students' writings) are as much about their relationships with texts—in this case, Hip Hop—as they are about the ability to read and write about (Hip Hop) texts. Because it was relevant and because they were able to connect to Hip Hop, our students were able to write meaningful reflections and engage in critical conversations about Hip Hop, which represent, in many ways, their words and their worlds.

The messy issues of language and intolerance in English language arts persist. We live in a linguistically intolerant society where everyone is pressured to bend to the supremacy of standard English. I am not against students gaining proficiency in standard English. Both of the writing examples I have chosen to share illustrate, to a degree, students' proficiency in standard English. Rather, the issue of linguistic intolerance in English education speaks to the narrow frame in which we present English language arts. Therefore, in addition to excluding a variety of language resources, we often exclude a variety of cultural resources, too. In doing so, we marginalize students who would benefit greatly from inclusive English language arts by default.

To avoid "explicitly" teaching students "edited " English (Delpit, 1988) and to help marginalized students gain the linguistic tools needed to succeed in American society, I have argued that the primacy of standard English/canonical text over other American languages/literatures creates linguistic/cultural divisions in English language arts which privilege the status quo. Our current approaches to English language arts and writing help to perpetuate exclusionary educational practices.

Furthermore, this work suggests that Hip Hop is effective in helping students meet national writing standards. As Morrell and Duncan-Andrade (2002) point out, "once learned, these analytic and interpretive tools developed through engagement with popular cultural texts can be applied to canonical texts as well." As illustrated here, students write about Hip Hop in ways that we desire for them to write about other texts. Since they are able to respond to Hip Hop in sophisticated ways, teachers should seriously consider using Hip Hop texts to help guide students on their journeys to become more successful writers.

REFERENCES

Appleman, D. (2000). *Critical encounters in high school English: Teaching literary theory to adolescents.* New York: Teachers College Press.

Brown, A. (2005, November). Using hip-hop in schools: Are we appreciating culture or raping rap? *The Council Chronicle.* National Council of Teachers of English: (http://www.ncte.org/pubs/chron/formembers/123024.htm).

Delpit, L. (1988). The silenced dialogue: Power and pedagogy in educating other people's children. *Harvard Educational Review, 58,* 280–298.

Derrida, J. (1976). *Grammatology.* Baltimore: The Johns Hopkins Press.

Derrida, J. (1982). *Margins of philosophy.* Chicago: The University of Chicago Press.

Dyson, A. H. (2003). *The brothers and sisters learn to write: Popular literacies in childhood and school cultures.* New York: Teachers College Press.

Fisher, M. T. (2003). Open mics and open minds: Spoken word poetry in African Diaspora Participatory Literacy Communities. *Harvard Educational Review, 73*(3), 362–389.

Freire, P., & Macedo, D. (1987). *Reading the word and the world.* Westport, CT: Bergin and Garvey.

Halliday, M.A.K. (1980). Three aspects of children's language development: Learning language, learning through language, learning about language. In Y. M. Goodman, M. M. Haussler, & D.S. Strickland (Eds.), *Oral and written language development research: Impact on the schools.* Proceedings of papers presented at National Council of Teachers of English and International Reading Association.

hooks, b. (1992). *Black looks: Race and representation.* Boston: South End Press.

Kailin, J. (2002). *Antiracist education: From theory to practice.* Lanham, MD: Rowman & Littlefield Publishers.

Kirkland, D. (2004). Rewriting school: Critical writing pedagogies for the secondary English classroom. *Journal of Teaching of Writing, 21*(1&2), 83–96.

Kirkland, D. E. (2005). *The power of their texts: Using hip hop to help urban students meet national standards for the English language arts.* Paper presented at the Annual Meeting of the National Council of Teachers of English.

Kirkland, D. E. (2006). *The boys in the hood: Exploring literacy in the lives of six urban adolescent Black males.* Unpublished dissertation, Michigan State University, East Lansing, MI.

Kitwana, B. (2003). *The hip hop generation: Young Black and crisis in African American culture.* New York: Basic Civitas.

Ladson-Billings, G. (1996). Lifting as we climb: The womanist tradition in multicultural education. In J. A. Banks (Ed.), *Multicultural education, transformative knowledge, and action: Historical and contemporary perspectives* (pp. 179–200). New York: Teachers College Press.

Light, A. (Ed.). (1999). *The vibe history of hip hop.* New York: Three Rivers Press.

Mahiri, J. (1998). *Shooting for excellence: African American and youth culture in new century schools.* New York: Teachers College Press.

Michigan Department of Education. (2003). *The Michigan Educational Assessment Program (MEAP) tests.* Retrieved January 22, 2005, from http://www.michigan .gov.mde/

Morgan, J. (1999). *When chickenheads come home to roost: My life as a hip hop feminist.* New York: Simon and Schuster.

Morrell, E., & Duncan-Andrade, J. M. R. (2002). Promoting academic literacy with urban youth through engaging hip-hop culture. *English Journal, 91,* 88–92.

Morrell, E. (2004). *Linking literacy and popular culture: Finding connections for lifelong learning.* Norwood, MA: Christopher-Gordon Publishers, Inc.

National Council of Teachers of English & International Reading Association. (1996). *Standards for the English language arts.* Urbana, IL & Newark, DE: Authors.

Pough, G. (2004). *Check it while I wreck it: Black womanhood, hip-hop culture and the public sphere.* Boston: Northeastern University Press.

Powell, C. T. (1991). Rap music: An education with a beat from the street. *Journal of Negro Education, 60*(3), 245–259.

Richardson, E. (2003). *African American literacies.* New York: The Free Press.

Rose, T. (1994). *Black noise: Rap music and black culture in contemporary America.* Middletown, CT: Wesleyan University Press.

Rosenblatt, L. (1968). *Literature as exploration* (2nd ed.). New York: Noble and Noble.

Rosenblatt, L. (1978). *The reader, the text, the poem: The transactional theory of the literary work.* Carbondale: Southern University Press.

Showalter, E. (1989). Toward a feminist poetics. In R. Con David & R. Schliefer (Eds.), *Contemporary literary criticism* (pp. 457–478). New York: Longman.

Smitherman, G. (1997). The chain remain the same: Communicative practices in the hip-hop nation. *Journal of Black Studies, 28,* 1, 3–25.

Smitherman, G. (1999). *Talkin' that talk.* New York: Routledge.

Wade, S. E., & Moje, E. B. (2000). The role of text in classroom learning. In M. L. Kamil, P. B. Mosenthal, P. D. Pearson, & R. Barr (Eds.), *Handbook of reading research* (Vol. 3). Mahwah, NJ: Erlbaum.

CHAPTER 10

BEYOND FORMULAS

Closing the Gap Between Rigid Rules and Flexible Strategies for Student Writing

Chris M. Anson

ABSTRACT

Too often, students learn static formulas for writing that do not readily transfer to the multiple, complex contexts and tasks they face as they cross the bridge to college and work. This chapter describes and theorizes a recursive process in which students collectively articulate criteria for writing assignments, internalize them, and then apply those to their own and others' developing texts. As we consider such ways to involve students in formative assessment, we also gain new insights into the design and support of our own assignments and our response and evaluation practices.

A dutiful student who nevertheless struggled with her classes in high school, Danelle has just begun her first semester at a mid-size state university that has been increasing its academic standards through new curricular outcomes. As Danelle faces her first college writing assignments, she tries to subdue her growing apprehension—that familiar fear of not knowing what her teachers want, of what to do or where to start on her assignments.

Closing the Gap, pages 147–164
Copyright © 2007 by Information Age Publishing
All rights of reproduction in any form reserved.

Her Western Civilization professor has asked the class to write an interpretive paper on the concept of property rights in early modern France, using the course materials and three Web-based sources. The three- to four-page paper has no other instructions except the warning that it should be an "interpretive essay," not a book report or a research paper. Meanwhile, Danelle's composition instructor has assigned a paper focusing on education, inspired by three readings discussed in class. The "short argumentative essay" is supposed to "provide support for assertions" through the use of "analysis and the explanation of evidence."

As she reads over these assignments, with their complex expectations for focus and genre, with their language of "critical analysis" and "interpretation" and "style appropriate to the occasion," Danelle feels baffled. By the end of her senior year of high school, she had finally begun to grasp the form of the five-paragraph essay, its all-important thesis standing out in her mind like a golden rule. She recalls how she had tried to follow the formula when she took the SAT writing test. She had developed three short paragraphs, each describing a different personal experience concerning conformity (the essay prompt), and then looped her conclusion back to her thesis statement that conformity could sometimes be a good thing. But now these longer papers, daunting in their structures and informational complexity, are making her 25-minute SAT essay seem like something from her distant childhood.

Danelle's story is not unique. It is repeated tens of thousands of times a year as students move from high school to college and try to transfer what they learn from one academic situation to the next. In many ways, the more formulaic their prior instruction, the greater their frustration, anxiety, or bewilderment when they try to map those formulas onto new tasks with new constraints, audiences, purposes, and expectations for specific genres.

This essay proposes a multi-staged instructional method designed to help students acquire strategic knowledge as writers—knowledge that can help them analyze new and sometimes unfamiliar writing tasks and their surrounding rhetorical situations. The method is based on a process of working toward criteria—textual or rhetorical standards—formatively and inductively. Although the method remains localized and task-specific, it is designed to be transportable to new settings and tasks. In this way, it replaces static formulas with a dynamic, strategic process that gives control of rhetorical and linguistic decisions to students and not to schemas often rote-learned and of little use.

THE PROBLEM OF CRITERIA

As any quick search for writing assignments on the Internet reveals, students often must write papers and reports with no explicit criteria for success beyond the trivia of font size and margin width. Typically, they must *infer* a successful performance from the provisions of the assignment and the usually subtle cues embedded in their teacher's admonitions and suggestions for how to complete the task. Early but still highly relevant scholarship in composition showed the need for students to take control of their work by using flexible strategies rather than rigid rules. For example, in an analysis of a "best case" scenario—an excellent teacher and a hard-working, eager student—Sperling and Freedman (1987) documented that performing well remains a mystery to even the most skilled students, who are reduced to the application of teacher-pleasing ruses or the ubiquitous guessing at "what the teacher wants." Mike Rose's (1984) work showed the origins of a writer's block and other cognitive difficulties in students' attempts to apply "rigid rules" to their writing; either they used inflexible plans inappropriate to an entire task, or they used plans at inappropriate times during the task. Students who did not suffer from writer's block used seventeen times as many functional strategies for writing as did those who had trouble.

For any novice writer, new genres and writing situations will create anxiety and lead to unproductive processes if they are not given strategies for figuring out what makes a good response to the task. Consider the following 12th-grade assignment, which is handed out with no accompanying criteria or evaluation standards. Students have just finished reading George Orwell's *1984.*

> Although the year 1984 has long since passed, Orwell was writing about a time that for him was well into the future. Think about the world that Orwell describes in the book as if he were describing a world in our own future—perhaps 2020 or 2030. Analyze our current society in terms of Orwell's vision. Do you think we are moving toward that vision? Do you see any signs that anything Orwell feared in 1984 have come to pass or are on the horizon? Choose some specific example(s) to illustrate your response; they could be from personal experience, from something you read or heard about in the news, or other information.

Students approaching this assignment may be challenged to draw on strategic composing knowledge in order to *analyze* their society using a novelist's creative vision. Perhaps they don't know exactly what analysis means in this context, or perhaps the analysis they learned in high school biology—understanding the relationship between the component organization and processes of an organism—won't help them to work out relationships between historical causes and effects or consider hypothetical eventualities by substituting moments in a string of actions. They also may be approaching an alien genre, an analytical paper that draws both on elements of a novel and on other information, perhaps from experience or external sources—a creature of unfamiliar features and unknown capabilities. Who is their audience? What purpose are they writing for? Are they trying to describe or persuade? Are they *extrapolating* from *1984* to create their own imagined world further in the future, or are they *extending* Orwell's vision? And if the latter, is it from Orwell's historical position, or Orwell as he might think at present, if he were still alive? Are they supposed to answer the tag questions directly ("Yes, we are moving toward Orwell's vision"), or are the questions simply rhetorical prompts to get them thinking?

To repair these lapses in support for students' work, many teachers offer a rubric or scoring guide—a condensed template of criteria designed to give them formative information about how their work will be assessed and then, in turn, serving the dual purpose of clarifying the summative criteria the teacher will use in assessing the final text. For the assignment above, imagine that students are given the following rubric used to gauge their performance (see Figure 10.1).

Clearly, a limited or unsupported assignment becomes more explicit with the addition of standards for success like these. But when we see the criteria again through the lens of novice writers approaching an unfamiliar task, they provide clarification only at a high level of abstraction, and thus are only marginally helpful. Without operational definitions of "thoughtful analysis" or "clear structure," students given this rubric will know that there are specific expectations for their writing, but not how to demonstrate those in their papers beyond the relatively simple matter of surface correctness. An "above average" score on their use of examples might give them some positive reinforcement, but that will not in itself help them to know what counts as the appropriate use of examples.

Criteria	Excellent	Above average	Average	Below average	Poor
Analysis is thoughtful and interesting					
Sufficient examples are used to support claims					
Essay has clear structure with smooth transitions					
Grammar, punctuation, spelling, etc., are correct					

Figure 10.1. Example of common grading rubric.

KNOWLEDGE OF GENRE
AND THE PROBLEM OF TRANSFER

Most learners bring elaborate knowledge of discourse into the classroom. If we hold up a copy of a paperback with a picture of a woman on a cliff by the seashore, drenched in moonlight, her somewhat transparent negligee gently blown by the ocean breeze, students will immediately tell us that the book is a romance novel. They will then explain some of the features of plot and language style that characterize the genre, showing that they recognize romance-novel writing when they see it and that they might even be able to create a brief parody of it if asked. This kind of internalized textual knowledge will be evident for many other kinds of writing familiar to students, including mysteries, editorials and news reports, advertisements, fables, Internet scam letters, textbook chapters, and five-paragraph themes. They have acquired this knowledge through exposure, sometimes consciously in classroom settings or discussions with friends, sometimes more tacitly and functionally.

As research has demonstrated, however, students exposed to new writing situations and new forms of text have difficulty transferring and acting on existing discourse knowledge. They don't know what counts as appropriate rhetorical and linguistic decisions (see Brown & Herndl, 1986; Anson & Forsberg, 1990), and they often end up creating texts that seem inappropriate to the situation, violating the expectations of readers who are part of the context. It is not that writers faced with a new rhetorical and textual situation forget all they know about discourse and are reduced to illiteracy; rather, they transfer knowledge only at low levels of text production (stringing words together into syntactically and semantically correct sentences, for example). In the absence of higher-level knowledge—knowledge of audience expectations, genre conventions, rhetorical and structural options, and choices of style or lexis—they may fall back on known genres and situations to complete the task. In more severe cases, even the presumably low-level, transferable abilities can be affected, leading to garbled sentences or a series of understandable sentences that together make up a garbled paragraph. Although the phenomenon of non-transferability is so obvious that it ought to be generally acknowledged and accepted, many people, including educators, are skeptical; they wonder why students can't simply learn to write effectively in a demanding English course and then perform well in all subsequent writing situations. For such skeptics to understand the validity of the transfer problem, they must themselves be placed into an unfamiliar context and asked to write successfully in a new genre for an audience whose expectations are unknown to them. (For an engaging account of seasoned university faculty members who experimentally took courses outside of their area of specialization and then tried to perform well in them, see Tobias, 1990.)

People placed into an unfamiliar writing context may recognize that what they have learned to do well—or with at least passable success—does not "work" to produce text there. Although discomfiting, this realization can give them reason to seek out the information they need: a set of procedures or processes for writing, models that give them glimpses of expected styles and formats, or mentors to guide their work and offer useful formative feedback. The more fully learners have been indoctrinated to believe in a static formula or set of rules that will apply to the universe of discourse, however, the more likely they are to avoid seeking out this additional knowledge, falling back on their now-inappropriate dicta to write their way into the new and unfamiliar. Even conscientious teachers who explain that a set of rules or a formula should be used only in certain situations know that students often ignore what is relativistic in a lesson and retain what is absolute. On the sentence level, such instruction often shows up in first-year college classrooms as ridiculous (or misinterpreted) pronouncements nevertheless etched into the consciousness of many freshmen: "Never use personal pronouns in your writing," "Never end a sentence with a verb," "Never begin a sentence with a preposition." Cured forever of the passive voice, the college student enrolled in a biology course will apply her rule to the displeasure of the lab-section coordinator and to the detriment of her own performance. By trial and error, she then unlearns the rule and relearns something about the passive voice: it *depends*. (For more on unlearning, see Harklau, Kay, & Siegal, 1999.)

INTERNALIZING CRITERIA

Expert writers often approach a new writing task or situation strategically, reflecting on fundamental rhetorical principles such as their purposes for writing, the audience they are addressing (or invoking), and the primary information or content they need to convey. They may consider genres whose characteristics they know well to see if elements of those genres might work in the new situation. They may begin formulating some language options—"turning on" certain stylistic considerations or the sounds and rhythms of certain kinds of sentences in their minds. These multiple possibilities—rhetorical, textual, pragmatic—will weave through their thinking as they plan their texts and begin writing (see Anson, 1999).

Novice writers, on the other hand, may begin by focusing all their attention on content or ideas without regard to form, style, or considerations of purpose or audience. Or they may become embroiled, as Mina Shaughnessy (1977) demonstrated, in sentence-level concerns, unable to move their ideas forward until they have tried to apply "rules" to their prose. If they have diligently memorized formulas, they may enact those consciously or unconsciously as they write, producing writing at odds with the expectations of their readers and context. How can we help such students to use the thinking and planning strategies of more skilled writers?

DEVELOPING CRITERIA COLLECTIVELY

It may be possible to tease from students some general ideas about what makes a "good" text in a given situation if they have had some prior experience as readers with the genre. They can be asked, for example, to explain the characteristics of a successful narrative, and most will offer some ideas with a little prompting. But typically these characteristics will remain at a high level of generality ("good narratives tell an interesting story") without creating links between the solicited standards and their manifestation in actual texts. The most important principle for helping students to internalize skills of judgment about various kinds of texts is to link generalized criteria or standards to the specific ways they do or don't show up in actual cases.

The collective development of criteria, therefore, relies on a movement between sample texts and statements that reflect judgments on those texts. For example, if students are working on narrative, they are first given copies of a sample narrative written by an anonymous student from a previous class, preferably in response to the same assignment. (Permissions should always be obtained from students in each class, most of whom will agree in writing to allow their work to be shared anonymously for future educational purposes.) It is important to choose samples that reflect both strengths and weaknesses—neither stellar nor seriously flawed performances should be used, since these don't lead to complex, productive discussions. The best samples are those that represent interesting issues of style, voice, content, audience awareness, and so on. Students can be asked to read and study the sample(s) as homework, and then take some time to refresh their memories about the drafts in class before the discussion begins.

Working in small groups or as a large class, students then critique each sample, articulating what works well or not well in it. At some point during the discussion of the sample's strengths and weaknesses, students are asked to move from the particulars of the case at hand to the general, deriving more abstract principles to answer the question, "What makes a good X" (in this case, a classroom-based narrative). The general principles are written on the board or a projector, and discussion deliberately ties them back to some specific feature in the text.

In a discussion of a sample narrative, students have read the following passage:

> I was cheerleading captain and I loved basketball. I put a lot of work into my cheerleading season. We had a great team spirit between the cheerleaders and the teammates. We stood behind the team from beginning to end. We led our crowd to great enthusiasm and spirit which I believe had a terrific effect on our team. (Anson & Schwegler, 2005, p. 84)

Clearly, this passage represents lackluster narrative, without the kind of specific details and visual appeal that readers value in this genre. Students working in groups will readily critique this aspect of the sample narrative, especially if they are given some prompts to focus their attention. From their critique of the specific text, they can then be induced to frame a general principle from their observations: "A successful narrative describes scenes effectively, drawing readers into the scene and helping them to share in an experience." Even the common principle of "show, don't tell," which may seem formulaic, is *internalized* through its connection to specific sentences and paragraphs in specific texts.

When students have come up with a comprehensive set of principles for good narratives, the teacher transcribes these and then, between classes, produces a written, draft version of the students' own standards, embellishing or modifying them to make them clear. In the subsequent class session, students receive the cleaned-up principles on a handout, which is clearly labeled as a draft in progress, and then the class applies them more systematically to one or more additional sample texts. As they "test" the criteria on further samples, they can add to, revise, particularize, or qualify the criteria. Because the students themselves are articulating and refining the principles, in a sense they "own" them, and can apply them more readily to new texts, further anchoring them to their tacit and conscious knowledge of the genre.

SUPPORTING LEARNING

As students work with sample texts and collectively create lists of criteria, they are constructing judgments and internalizing standards mainly as *readers*. As they begin working on their own narratives, however, they may find that what makes a paper "good" is more easily said than done. The gap between recognizing criteria for success and realizing these criteria in their own prose often remains the least effectively resolved problem in writing instruction.

As a follow-up to the collaborative development of criteria, students can begin working *formatively* with each of the standards, through supporting lessons and drafting activities. For example, if the class decides that good narratives contain lively description, class activities can focus on how to draft prose that meets this criterion. Students can work on brief passages individually and then share these in small groups, further applying their judgments to each other's drafts and making suggestions for improvements. At some point, however, it may be necessary to begin systematically unpacking the (usually generalized) criteria. This decision will be based on an assessment of the students' proficiency at more specific levels within the criteria. If students are having trouble "describing scenes effectively," for example, then further work with this criterion—and more iterative practice with its components—may be productive.

As illustration, consider the basic criteria one class created for effective narratives using a sample student paper.

A good narrative:
- Describes scenes effectively
- If present, uses dialogue authentically
- Uses action to move the narrative forward
- Has some kind of main conflict that needs to be resolved
- Implies a "point" without coming right out and saying what it is

Although they have identified a criterion from something done well or not well in the sample paper, they need to move from identification to production. If they don't know how to describe scenes effectively (or what this means in terms of linguistic choices), then the class can be asked to brainstorm more specific features of the criterion—"how we know it when we see it"—at more and more specific levels:

The effective description of scene comes *from*:

- the use of rich, descriptive language
- attention to relevant, interesting details

Rich, descriptive language *comes from*:

- strong, active verbs
- evocative but not overused adjectives
- variety of word choice

The "unpacking" of criteria in this way allows the overall strategy to be tuned to the abilities of each specific class, scaffolding on existing knowledge at an appropriate level of recognition and text production. The depth of specification and practice will also depend on how familiar the genre is to students; it may be possible to stop at a relatively high level in writing a narrative, for example, but not in writing a persuasive editorial for a local newspaper.

Although it is tempting to give such sets of criteria to students and tell them to be mindful of them when they write, *the students must always generate the criteria themselves.* This requires patience for repetition as class after class of students come up with what will often be similar criteria. The "cleaned up" versions should always reflect the work of that particular class, and should honor its own language by not straying too far from what they had originally produced. This principle is crucial: for students to internalize criteria, they must be able to articulate them in their own language and on their own terms. The teacher becomes a kind of conduit, ensuring that the students collectively agree on the criteria and recording them in a form that all can understand and use.

TURNING CRITERIA FORMATIVE

After students have articulated general criteria based on sample texts and work with these criteria to recognize how they are manifested in specific textual characteristics, they can then turn the general criteria to use working on their own drafts. Peer-group response find support in a robust body of literature, both scholarly and pedagogical, but with a few exceptions, little work has demonstrated the importance of linking response and revision to careful and systematic work with evaluation criteria. Typically, students are given revision guides that contain questions aimed at making sure they adhere to various requirements or apply general principles to their ongoing drafts ("Is the essay well organized?" or "Does the writer present a clear thesis somewhere at the beginning of the paper?"). Without a deeper understanding of concepts like "organization," or an awareness that theses can take several forms and placements, students often participate in response groups perfunctorily, and their revised essays show little improvement because they have not *deeply* applied the criteria embedded in the revision questions.

Because students themselves have expressed criteria for successful essays at the start of the process, they will be more eager and well prepared to apply these during response groups. Questions can be designed to encourage more discussion about specific textual features. For example, instead of asking whether a narrative "describes scenes effectively," a question might push students to analyze what characteristics, especially of those previously discussed in class, create a more effectively described scene. Because the students already have the language for this analysis, their peer-group responses—and ultimately their revisions—will be far more effective and will engage them in more serious, sustained, and productive discussions.

Considering the Application of Criteria

As students revise and refine their papers, they will become more concerned about how their final products will be evaluated, at least if their performance is being graded or counted in some way. In many instructional settings, students perceive a disjunction between the instruction they receive and the process by which their work is evaluated. They often believe that teachers' evaluations are subjective, mysterious, and disconnected from what they are told in the classroom.

A final stage in the creation and use of criteria involves "annotated models" to help students see how the criteria are applied. Although students already will have applied the criteria to sample drafts, this stage is an opportunity to show them how an expert evaluator reaches similar conclusions. Having produced a version of the class-generated criteria that is purely evaluative, perhaps tied to a grading scale, the instructor makes that version available to the students so they can see how their own standards will be applied by an expert evaluator to their work. Again, the instructor chooses an interestingly problematic sample paper. He or she then annotates the paper—usually in the margins—with commentary designed both to evaluate the sample and to explain the reasons for the evaluative judgments, so that students get a window into the teacher's response and reasoning. This strategy can be done with simple marginal comment on a clean version of a paper, which is then photocopied for the class. In more elaborate versions of the method, teachers create Web pages in which students first read the entire sample paper with no comments. They then choose one of the criteria that they have collectively created; this link opens a duplicate of the paper with highlighted words and phrases. As the students pass their cursor over these highlights or click on them, windows open containing explanatory commentary. Further criteria open new versions of the paper annotated from that perspective. In our example of the narrative, the criterion, "describes scenes effectively" is explained in the context of a passage from a student's narrative describing the passing of his grandmother (see Figure 10.2). The highlighted line, "The house was gloomy," has opened a popup window that calls attention to the need for more specific details, especially visual images, that could evoke a sense of sadness in the writer's intended audience. The popup window reads:

> Although as readers we get the general sense of sadness and a kind of gloomy feeling from the passage, it lacks the specific details that make a narrative

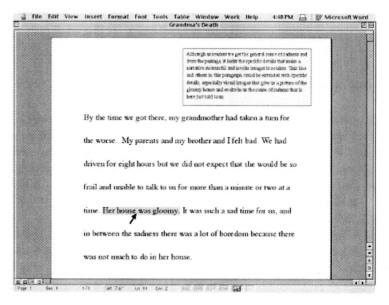

Figure 10.2.

successful and invoke images in readers. This line and others in this paragraph could be extended with specific details, especially visual images that give us a picture of the gloomy house and evoke in us the sense of sadness that is here just told to us.

Although it is possible to annotate a single document and label or code each annotation to a particular criterion, separate versions allow students to see the sample document through a single lens. They can then see how individual characteristics of a text contribute to its success or shortcomings. Annotations can also provide more detail than is typically possible in a quickly evaluated paper, on which the teacher has selectively commented.

INTRODUCING UNFAMILIAR GENRES

The preceding interconnected strategies, pivoting as they do on students' own articulation of standards based on analyses of sample papers, works well with genres familiar to students; they bring to bear on their analyses considerable experience as readers of similar kinds of texts. But what happens when we want to introduce a new and perhaps unfamiliar genre to students and have them write papers in that genre? If they have little or no prior experience reading or writing such texts, how can they begin to make critical judgments on the quality and nature of samples?

In such cases, students will need to be introduced to the genre more slowly and explicitly, with information about its typical contexts and purposes, expectations about its style, voice, and structure, and strategies for representing its content. Successful models of the genre are important here for students to experience as readers. As they become more accustomed to some of the features of the genre, they can then begin to make judgments on samples that represent various interesting problems and issues, as described earlier.

In addition, even familiar genres vary considerably across contexts because genres themselves are socially constructed and not stable entities (see Miller, 1984). The "personal experience narrative" is a typical classroom genre but it is connected to many other kinds of academic and professional narrative forms such as memoir, travel writing, ethnographies, and certain kinds of nonfiction essays. As students learn strategies for one kind of narrative, then, they can be introduced to variations and other manifestations of narrative, working through the cycle of criteria-building and the application of these criteria to essays-in-progress.

The processes thus far described can be built into a course as cycles of activity. Figure 10.3 shows the first cycle, using the familiar example of the personal experience narrative. In this cycle, sample student texts are used to help students generate their own criteria for what counts as a successful narrative. Notice that the resulting criteria may be incomplete, or some general criteria may not have many further, detailed criteria that explain them. The sample texts may bring to the surface only some features of narrative writing. For this reason, sets of criteria can be presented as "under construction" and able to be modified or refined.

After working to articulate criteria and testing them in further sample narratives, students enter into the second cycle, shown in Figure 10.4. This cycle involves operationalizing those criteria in drafts and revisions (with support from peer commentary, revision guides, and further classroom discussion). Here, the teacher has turned the student-generated criteria into a revision guide used in peer conferences. Notice that the questions or actions in the peer revision guide embed the levels of detail in various strategic ways (for example, the "meta-question" in #2—"Decide how effectively the narrative describes a scene"—is made operational through specific actions: mark all cases of rich, descriptive language (looking for strong, active verbs) and put a "naught" symbol next to verbs that seem weak and inactive. As students work with their own and others' drafts, they can note issues or features of their narratives that lead to further refinement of the criteria (and, if desired, the questions on the revision guide). Perhaps the overuse of strong, active verbs (such as replacing every "be" verb) makes the narrative too forced or overwritten; this criterion, then, becomes more sophisticated, and a qualification about overuse can be

Cycle 1:

Student groups read and critique a sample student narrative	⇒	Whole-class follow-up turns critique into draft criteria	⇒	Teacher prepares full draft of criteria for the class

Example of class-generated first draft of criteria for "good narratives":

describes scenes effectively	uses rich, descriptive language	strong, action verbs
		careful use of adjectives
		variety in word choice
	uses relevant, interesting details	details add to sense of being "in" the scene
		details do not bog down the progress of the narrative
uses action to move the narrative forward	develops each part of the incident evenly	
	structures chronologically or with the use of flashbacks	
has some kind of main conflict or event that gets the reader interested	introduces tension or a sense of "plot" around an event	
	event is interesting to most readers	
has an appropriate point of view	point of view does not judge for the reader	
	point of view stays consistent	uses the same tense in narration
		stays the same distance from the events
if present, uses dialogue effectively	interaction seems natural	
	dialogue is broken up into new paragraphs	
	action and dialogue are interspersed	

Figure 10.3.   First cycle—drafting criteria.

Cycle 2:

Students apply draft of criteria to more samples and refine	Teacher creates a revision guide for peer conferences	Students apply revision guide to own and peers' drafts

Example of first revision guide using student-generated criteria for good narratives:

Here are the criteria we developed for good narratives, turned into questions for our peer revision conference. Please read your partners' drafts and, for each, fully answer each of the questions below in preparation for the peer conference.

1. Describe the main conflict or event that gets the reader interested. Try to locate one or more places in the paper where there is a sense of tension or the start of a plot. Say whether you, as a reader, are interested in the event(s) being described.

2. Describe the point of view that the writer takes toward the event(s). Try to find a metaphor or descriptive word for that point of view ("detached," "angry," "passionate," "uncaring," "feels like the writer is trying to make me see the scene in only one way," etc. Put a note in the margin at any point where you think the point of view shifts or changes unnecessarily or disruptively. Circle any problematic tense shifts or changes in how distant the writer is from the event(s).

3. Decide how effectively the narrative describes a scene. Put a line to the margin and use an exclamation point for all cases of rich, descriptive language (especially strong, active verbs, carefully used adjectives, and variety in word choice). Do the same, but use a "naught" symbol (?) next to weak, inactive verbs that could be replaced, problematic adjectives, and dull, repetitive choice of words. Next, look for details, and note any that are especially effective or ineffective, as well as details that don't contribute to the narrative and seem to "bog it down."

4. Sketch a simple outline of events in order to show how the paper uses action to move the story forward. Note how much time is spent on each part and decide if this is effective. Note whether the narrative moves chronologically, or, if it does not, whether the result is deliberate or effective (as in flashbacks) or confusing.

5. If dialogue is used, decide how effective it is. Does it seem natural and authentic? Is it rendered effectively, with appropriate paragraph breaks? Is the weaving together of dialogue and action effective? Identify places in the draft where dialogue is used effectively or ineffectively.

6. *Keep notes on any other features you discuss or notices that are not on our criteria. We will modify the criteria as we work through the drafts.*

Figure 10.4.   Second cycle—operationalizing criteria in peer conferences.

added to it. In this way, the criteria continue to be refined, both on paper and in students' internalized understanding of what makes a good paper, as they notice more features or as the original features become more complex and nuanced.

Cycle 3:

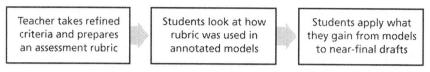

Figure 10.5.   Third cycle—moving toward summative application of criteria.

Finally, as students revise their work for submission, they need to move from the formative use of criteria to summative application of the criteria to their own writing. Annotated models, like the one shown in Figure 10.2, can help students to see both the validity of the criteria they have created and the way those criteria are used instructionally to determine a grade or other assessment on one or more final student texts. This third cycle is shown in Figure 10.5.

As we consider all three cycles together, it soon becomes clear that they are recursive both internally and with one another. As students grapple with the question of what makes a text "good" in response to an assignment, it is essential that they move between student examples (again, preferably ones that have both strengths and weaknesses) and criteria, between continuously refined criteria and their own and peers' writing, and between criteria seen from a summative perspective, already assessed work, and their own drafts in progress. The recursive interaction of the three cycles is shown in Figure 10.6.

Notice also that as students work with, internalize, and act on new awareness of discursive standards or reader expectations, they can map that awareness onto new variations in the genre they have been writing. For example, what makes a classroom narrative "good" also applies to certain kinds of reviews, such as a restaurant review. But narrativity in a restaurant review is much more muted than in a personal experience narrative; the focus is on the events of the meal and its surroundings, though filtered through the impressions and consciousness of the reviewer. Artful teaching will help students to take what they already know about good narratives and begin bending or stretching or adapting it to a new genre or subgenre that makes use of a narrative quality.

TOWARD STRATEGIC THINKING AND PLANNING

When students learn formulaic approaches to writing, they often find it difficult to apply those formulas to new writing tasks, contexts, and audiences. Writing is persistently stereotyped as a monolithic skill that can be learned effectively in high school and then simply "called up" in further writing sit-

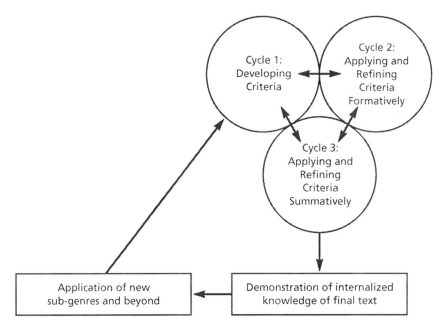

Figure 10.6.   Recursive interaction of the cycles.

uations in college and beyond. This inaccurate view of writing is responsible for countless (and enduring) complaints that teachers or administrators or schools have failed to prepare students to meet the demands of complex tasks.

Just as students must be urged away from static formulas and encouraged to think strategically about writing, so teachers much stop relying on "canned" materials in their own instruction. When we develop criteria with students for writing tasks in our classrooms, we must accept the idea that we are developing localized standards for assessment. We must have faith that, through iterations of work with the criteria, they will continue to develop and encompass more of those characteristics we associate with successful performance. Just as it is essential that students themselves generate these ideas, so it is essential for teachers to stop using vague rubrics and predigested materials and rely instead on the active *creation* of knowledge with students.

The strategies described in this chapter are designed to model for students some productive ways to approach new writing tasks and situations. But the problem of transfer does not rest only on those teachers in Context A, such as senior high school, from which students will move into Context B; it rests as well on teachers in Context B—and C, and D. If teachers in all disciplines can help students to recognize, practice, and make judgments on the standards that define the particular genres and occasions for writing that they assign, students will continue to internalize the principles of effective texts and build on their repertoire of rhetorical and linguistic strategies for further writing. This will require more energy among many faculty in defining and clarifying their own expectations, as suggested by Bob Broad (2003) in a process called "dynamic criteria mapping." At some point, of course, students will find themselves facing an unfamiliar task in a new and bewildering context; but having been led through the processes of identifying those qualities that make successful texts of various kinds, they will be better prepared—as expert writers are—to seek out the kind of strategic information that will help them to write effectively as quickly as possible in their new settings.

REFERENCES

Anson, C. M. (1999). Talking about writing: A classroom-based study of students' reflections on their drafts. In J. B. Smith & K. Yancey (Eds.), *Student self-assessment and development in writing* (pp. 59–74). Cresskill, NJ: Hampton.

Anson, C. M., & Forsberg, L. L. (1990). Moving beyond the academic community: Transitional stages in professional writing. *Written Communication, 7,* 200–231.

Anson, C. M., & Schwegler. R. A. (2005). *The Longman handbook for writers and readers* (4th ed.). New York: ABLongman.

Broad, B. (2003). *What we really value: Beyond rubrics in teaching and assessing writing.* Logan: Utah State University Press.

Brown, R. L., & Herndl, C. G. (1986). An ethnographic study of corporate writing: Job status as reflected in written text. In B. Couture (Ed.), *Functional approaches to writing: Research perspectives* (pp. 11–28). London: Frances Pinter.

Harklau, L., Kay, L., & Siegal, M. (Eds.). (1999). *Generation 1.5 meets college composition: Issues in the teaching of writing to U.S.-educated learners of ESL.* Mahwah, NJ: Lawrence Erlbaum.

Miller, C. R. (1984). Genre as social action. *Quarterly Journal of Speech, 70,* 151–176.

Rose, M. (1984). *Writer's block: The cognitive dimension.* Carbondale: Southern Illinois University Press.

Shaughnessy, M. P. (1977). *Errors and expectations: A guide for the teacher of basic writing.* New York: Oxford University Press.

Sperling, M,. & Freedman, S. W. (1987). A good girl writes like a good girl: Written response to student writing. *Written Communication, 4*(4), 343–369.

Tobias, S. (1990). *They're not dumb, they're different: Stalking the second tier.* Tucson, AZ: Research Corporation.

AFTERWORD

Success and the Status Quo

William Thelin

This volume has presented its readers with a number of pedagogical strategies to secure student investment and increase critical awareness. Many of the contributors understand the importance of contextualizing students' learning experiences, whether that understanding takes the form of accounting for the culture from which the students come or bridging the gap between writing for high school and writing for college. Some contributors focused on teacher education and the application of lessons in the high school classroom. At the base of these collaborations and innovations, however, is a progressive stance on the meaning of success. It is here I would like to linger.

Too often, various commissions or politicians will talk about the ills of education and announce or imply that a back-to-the-basics approach is necessary. The key word springing from No Child Left Behind is "accountability." While the state virtually ignores the ravages of unchecked capitalism on our cities, environment, and federal deficit—not to mention the countries our troops currently occupy—government seems intent on interfering with education. Teachers across the country would certainly welcome funding if it were offered, but the mandate, instead, seems to be to improve with the budget the schools already have and to shape curriculum in such a way as to pass reductive tests. Further, even though many of our schools have to use metal detectors to ensure the safety of both students and teachers, government involvement assumes, apparently, that education takes place in isolation from the culture around it, that poverty, vio-

Closing the Gap, pages 165–171
Copyright © 2007 by Information Age Publishing
All rights of reproduction in any form reserved.

lence, the necessity of at least two full-time incomes for most homes, the lure of drugs, the accelerated physical maturity of children, malnutrition, and health problems exacerbated by pollution and other toxins do not impact students' experience in school. The state wants to treat the symptoms rather than the illness itself. If we were to look hard to find some soundness in a back-to-basics approach, what chance would it stand given the forces it is up against?

*   *   *

Akron, Ohio, where I live, is faced with a budget crisis in its public school system. A number of levies have been attempted, but given the depressed economy in this region of the country, taxpayers have grown tired of supporting the schools just to keep them treading water, so to speak. While some citizens simply react to any levy or tax that they see taking money from their paychecks, the prevailing strand of thought focuses on the system itself. Levies cannot fix a damaged system. How much more additional resources should they send to schools that maintain a dropout rate of more than 20%? Shouldn't the system be shored up?

The result of voter conflict on the levies is that several schools have been closed. Students were relocated to other districts. The teacher to student ratio increased across the city. In the spring of 2006, even after these cutbacks, voters yet again cast ballots against a levy designed to ensure that existing schools did not have to cut programs. While accusations flew back and forth among citizens of wealthier and poorer districts that this district failed to bring out the vote or that district voted against its own self-interests, children soon felt the effects. Programs from foreign language to music were axed.

The children are not unaware of the choices being made for them. My daughter, Katrina, is all of 13 years old as of this writing. She hates the proficiency exams the schools force her to take and feels bored when she perceives the lesson plan in front of her as designed to teach to the test. I sense that her teachers voice their resentment to the students, as Katrina knows how her teachers' hands are tied and what they are giving up in order to meet the expectations of the test. Katrina is rightly worried about her future, as are her friends.

The anger Katrina and her friends feel can target prominent political figures. They do not understand President Bush's priorities and rail against him in the way we might expect from teenagers. Governor Taft's policies are the fodder for jokes. Yet, the president and governor are too distant for critique and protest, and Katrina and her friends do not know much about the local politicians and the history of the city. The main targets of their anger—I dare call it "rage" at times—are other children whom they perceive as privileged in some way. For example, while the performing arts program at Katrina's school was cut, her friends at the publicly supported performing arts academy still enjoy the benefits of such a program, although losing other programs. What used to be a friendly, perhaps spirited, rivalry between the schools and the children has deteriorated into jealousy and bitterness. I usually hear Katrina's snide remarks about the other school's children only when she is with friends attending her own school. The other day, however, I witnessed firsthand the increasing tension, as a discussion between Katrina and a friend, Rachel, escalated into a serious argument into which I needed to intervene. They wanted, in essence, to blame each other for what was cut from their schools. The ideology that has led to the financial problems lacks the concreteness needed for the two of them to focus on it. Instead, they point fingers at each other, cutting into friendship and damaging the potential for joint alliances and civic action. They are both afraid that they will not receive the benefit of a full education that they, ironically enough, will be left behind with only a grasp of the basic subjects and no nourishment of their talents and dreams.

*   *   *

Given the society into which students will enter, how do we define success? What do we want students to learn in our classrooms? What do we hope they achieve once they finish their education? Building on Arlette Ingram-Willis and Catherine D. Hunter's chapter in this book, I want to suggest that teaching to help students integrate smoothly into the status quo should not be our collective goal, both as high school and college instructors. Willis and Hunter's stated purpose in their teaching education courses is to create a "more socially just nation of literacy users," and they actively challenge the preconceived notions of the candidates in their English methods' classes, making use of multicultural literature to "encourage social justice and equity." Like many of the contributors to this volume, Willis and Hunter desire to teach future educators to challenge conventions of the status quo.

I applaud these efforts. Yet, I want to comprehend the complexity of challenging the status quo. In looking at co-editor Karen Keaton Jackson's contribution to this book, I see the contradictions in students' lives spelled out clearly. We educate students toward monetary success, but in trying to help them acquire the standard dialect with a vague goal of financial achievement, we ignore the erasure of their identity. Jackson's use of hip hop enlivened a class session she taught, teaching the students about the world around them. The pity, of course, is that she had only one class session with this particular group of students, but clearly the teaching honored the students' culture while critiquing practices that perpetuate a cycle of disempowerment. In this one session, students reacted to values that both embrace and reject the status quo. The rapper Nas, whose work I must confess I am ignorant of, presents the students with an understanding of African history that denies second-class status to African-Americans but warns against the lure of sloth, of drugs, of desiring sexual maturity too quickly, values with which most conservatives would agree. The students' writing reflected attempts at conforming to the standard dialect, which interests me because the samples provided by Jackson reflect a standard account of the American Dream. The radical critique provided by Nas is missing. Yet, can I say with any degree of integrity that bestowing these types of goals on a marginalized population is inappropriate or contrary to a radical critique?

So I wonder about the complexity of success and our mission as teachers. Countering the endullment students experience in school, to borrow a term from Ira Shor, has to mean something in the broader scheme of things. Efforts such as those documented in separate chapters here by Chris Anson, Kia Jane Richmond, and the collaboration between Hephzibah Roskelly and Kathleen J. Ryan to bridge gaps between high school and college writing classrooms matter. They cannot and should not be dismissed. But if we are able to invest our students in their learning and overcome the discord between different teaching environments as our students mature into adults, have we succeeded? Our students will be moving into a world teetering on a shaky foundation, one that has been overcome with consumerist competition, one where nations must try to develop nuclear-destructive capacity in order to secure the ability to make independent decisions, one where limited resources are thought to be (if actions reflect thought) limitless, one where lust and greed have replaced love and compassion. How do we reconcile our students' ambitions with the horror in front of them? Where do we locate success in our teaching?

*   *   *

Every fall, I teach the TA Practicum at the University of Akron. Some of my students have previous teaching experience. Several have come from Education programs. Most have earned a degree in English, either at the University of Akron or at a surrounding university. The issue that surfaces every semester revolves around the goals of our first-year composition program. Many TAs believe that teaching rhetorical craft, if not grammatical correctness, remains our primary duty. While not ignoring essential instruction in audience awareness, organization, style, and voice, I lead discussions on critical analysis over and above everything else. I unabashedly promote a curriculum that challenges the societal and pedagogical status quo and contextualize the TAs' teaching in political controversies that abound. The ethics of inserting the instructor's values into a classroom often get raised. Should we not be teaching skills free and clear of political commitment? Should we not always strive to achieve objectivity and fairness in our evaluation? Obviously, there are no easy answers to these questions. Recently, however, I thought the dialogue achieved a level of elevation that I will reproduce in a ficitionalized account here.

"Dr. Thelin, I should be able to grade any student opinion without taking into consideration my beliefs."

"What if it is an uninformed opinion?"

"As long as the student supports it."

"What if you know contrary facts?"

"That shouldn't matter."

"Really?" And this wasn't my voice this time. Another student had questioned this assertion. "Don't we have a responsibility to society? Aren't we educating, supposedly, the leaders of tomorrow? How can we not challenge them?"

"But I want to be fair," the first TA insisted. "I am imposing my values upon the students if I offer facts that the students must account for. What about those that I don't know? What about those that contradict what I believe?"

I'm not a guru. I don't pretend to be. But I reached a moment of clarity. "If to grade a student fairly," I said, "I must suppress my knowledge, and I must pretend that as a reader I am unaffected by statements I know not to be true, I am not, ultimately, grading the student fairly. I am capitulating to an ideology that believes content is divorced from form. I am enforcing a dogma that privileges expression over societal good. I am making the most profound statement I could possibly make in favor of the status quo."

"Are you saying we're being irresponsible if we don't promote a political belief in our classroom?"

"No, I'm saying that responsibility as a teacher involves having commitment to society. You are being political whatever you do, and you must come to terms with this. Our personal beliefs might turn out to be wrong. Polemics, therefore, have no place in the classroom. But in grappling with issues and encouraging students not to repeat the platitudes of the dominant society, we're asking them to revise in ways that will turn them into better writers and thinkers than if we take a hands-off approach. We must educate ourselves while we are educating our students and learn with them. Rhetoric and truth are intertwined."

"But if we teach the grammar and skills necessary toward clear expression, aren't we paving the way for knowledge? Won't our students learn about the world in other classes?"

"I believe in hope," I said. "I do not think 'hope' is a synonym for 'wishful thinking.' The leaders in our society are educated. Judging by the policies they promote, they were not educated critically. Educated people have done more damage to the world than the uneducated. If I am to give students skills without instruction in values, I am making a mistake that the great classical rhetoricians recognized. Language is powerful. Language shapes our society. We have a huge task in front of us as instructors of writing. We cannot shirk from our duties."

Some TAs believe I am one of the professors who should be on David Horowitz's infamous list of transgressors of legitimate academic inquiry. Others wrestle with the enormity of what I am suggesting. Others manage to shrug it off as they teach their classes. If we define "success" as having something to do with helping students understand the broader context of their education, there are no prescriptions to give our students. Success varies. Perhaps it can take place in that classroom relying on skills and drills, if a student with a progressive agenda uses the course to work for social justice. But can we merely hope for such an outcome instead of acting toward it?

*   *   *

Many of the contributors to this volume referenced Paulo Freire, and I do not want to sleight any of them as I conclude. Yet, I was most struck by the experiences of Kevin Salamone, who I will describe as a "returning teacher," in his collaboration with his mentor, Patricia Ruggiano Schmidt. Salamone left his career as a software developer to become a middle school teacher. Salamone bridged the gap between mandated state curriculum and the background of his students. In so doing, I think that he bridged a gap between his love of literature and his students' lives. But his impact on their lives is so much greater than he could possibly document in the pages given to him. He sees community and parental involvement as crucial. He acknowledges what his students bring to the classroom and uses it to enrich the curriculum. While I am sure it can be argued about the extent he pushes his agenda and the lack of a revolutionary feature, I believe he fosters the critical growth necessary for civic literacy and awareness, the type that acknowledges the conflicts and contradictions stemming from the dominant culture, the type for which Freire advocated. In this, I see success.

Success has to be contextualized. In a utopian society in which suffering was kept to a minimum and the gains of one nation did not come at the deprivation of another, certain types of literacy practices might be deemed as acceptable—others unacceptable. But we must keep our present day society in mind. The rapid changes we see often do not disturb the foundation, a foundation that serves the few at the expense of the many. We are living in a time that is violent to those who work the hardest. It is more violent still to those we do not frequently see—the people of color who have been and are victims of imperialism, the masses who starve, the distant countries that go without resources so that we can live in luxury. Success cannot be realized on a foundation so corrupt. It is only with genuine concern for the "other" that we can truly call our teaching successful. With this concern will come change. Only this can we call "success."

ABOUT THE CONTRIBUTORS

Chris M. Anson is University Distinguished Professor and Director of the Campus Writing and Speaking Program at North Carolina State University in Raleigh, North Carolina. He received his Ph.D. from Indiana University in English Language with a specialization in composition studies. Before joining NC State in 1999, he spent fifteen years at the University of Minnesota, where he directed the Program in Composition from 1988 to 1996 and was Morse-Alumni Distinguished Teaching Professor. He has published twelve books and over sixty articles on writing, teaching, and literacy development and has given over 325 lectures, conference papers, and workshops across the U.S. and in seventeen foreign countries. His professional summary may be found at the following URL: http://www.home.earthlink.net/~theansons/ Portcover.html.

Amy M. Goodburn is Associate Dean of the College of Arts and Sciences and an Associate Professor of English and Women's Studies at the University of Nebraska-Lincoln (1223 Oldfather Hall, Lincoln, NE, 68588-0312). She received her Ph.D. in 1994 from The Ohio State University in Composition and Rhetoric. Goodburn's research interests include teacher research and development, multicultural pedagogies, and ethnographic and community-based literacies. She coedited *Composition, Pedagogy, and the Scholarship of Teaching* (with Deborah Minter) and has published in nine edited collections and journals such as *English Education, JAC, WPA,* and *Composition Studies.* She also co-coordinates The Peer Review of Teaching Project.

Catherine D. Hunter earned her B. A. from Oberlin College, Oberlin and an M. Ed., Curriculum & Instruction at the University of Illinois at Urbana-Champaign. She is a former English teacher who is currently working on a doctorate in Language and Literacy at the University of Illinois at Urbana

Closing the Gap, pages 173–177
Copyright © 2007 by Information Age Publishing

Champaign. Her publications include a book review "African-Centered Pedagogy: Developing Schools of Success for African American Children" in *Journal of Curriculum Studies* (along with L. Buckley, J. Connor, and S. Williams) and co-author of a forthcoming book, *On Critically Conscious Research: Approaches to Language and Literacy Research,* with A. Willis, M. Montovan, L. Burke, L., A. Herrera, A. and H. Hall.

Karen Keaton Jackson is an assistant professor of English at North Carolina Central University in Durham, North Carolina where she teaches a variety of composition courses and directs the Writing Studio. She received her B.S. in English Secondary Education from Hampton University and her M.A. and Ph.D. in Composition and Rhetoric from Wayne State University. Her research interests include literacy, race, and identity, and how they intertwine in the urban writing classroom. As a graduate student, she taught courses in African-American literature, multicultural literacy, and helped to develop a community based service-learning course. Her recent publications include "The Compositionist as 'Other': A Critical Self-Reflection of an Instructor of Color in an Urban Service-Learning Classroom" in the edited collection *Social Change in Diverse Teaching Contexts: Touchy Subjects and Routine Practices.* She also is on the executive board for the Southeastern Writing Center Association.

David E. Kirkland is an assistant professor of English education at the Steinhardt School of Education at New York University. Kirkland received a Ph.D. in curriculum, teaching, and educational policy from Michigan State University. His work includes "Rewriting School: Critical Writing Pedagogies for the Secondary English Classroom," which was published in *the Journal of Teaching Writing.* His work and publications focus broadly on literacy, race, gender and urban education. He is recipient of several awards, including the Conference on College Composition and Communication *Scholars for the Dream Award.* His current project, "The Boys in the Hood: Exploring Literacy in the Lives of Adolescent Black Boys," is an ethnographic study that examines the challenges of acquiring literacy in urban Black America.

April Lambert is a M.A. student in composition and rhetoric at the University of Nebraska-Lincoln. She received her undergraduate degree in English, Spanish, and Education and spent a year teching high school at a rural high school. Her research interests include teacher identity development, literacy development, and critical literacies.

Matthew Kilian McCurrie is Assistant Professor of English at Columbia College, Chicago where he teaches a variety of writing courses, coordinates departmental assessment, and directs the literacy program. Prior to his arrival at Columbia, he was an assistant professor of English Education at Louisiana State University where he directed the LSU Writing Project. His published essays have appeared in journals like *Pedagogy, Composition Studies*, and *English Journal.*

Kia Jane Richmond is in her sixth year as an Assistant Professor of English at Northern Michigan University in Marquette, Michigan. She co-directs the English Education program and teaches courses in English Methods, Composition, Young Adult Literature, and Humanities. Richmond's articles have appeared in various scholarly journals including *English Education, Composition Studies, Issues in Writing*, and *Journal of the Assembly for Expanded Perspectives on Learning.*

Hephzibah Roskelly is Professor of English at the University of North Carolina at Greensboro, where she teaches courses in composition and rhetoric, American literature, and pedagogy. Before coming to UNCG, she was an assistant professor at the University of Massachusetts, Boston. She received her Ph.D. from the University of Louisville with specialization in rhetoric and composition. Research interests include gender and education, pragmatism and composition, and nineteenth century women's activism. Recent publications include "Everyday Use: Rhetoric at Work in Reading and Writing" (with David Joliffe) and "Breaking into the Circle: The Uses of Groups for Transforming the English Classroom."

Kathleen J. Ryan is an Assistant Professor of English and the Director of Composition at the University of Montana. Prior to directing Montana's program, Kate was the Undergraduate Writing Coordinator at West Virginia University and taught courses in English Education and college composition teaching. She earned her Ph.D. in Rhetoric and Composition at the University of North Carolina, Greensboro. Her research interests include teacher preparation, feminist rhetorival studies, and writing program administration. Her publications have appeared in *Rhetoric Society Quarterly, Composition Studies*, and *WPA: Journal of the Council of Writing Program Coordinators.*

Kevin Salamone was a software developer in Boston for fifteen years. As he made his daily commute by train with several colleagues in the field, he noticed that they immersed themselves in trade journals, the *Wall Street Journal* and PC magazines. He however read Steinbeck, Joyce and other classics. Subsequently, he realized that his heart was longing for a different profession and that was education. Therefore, he proceeded to get his provisional teaching certificate for Secondary English and that led to his family's move to his wife's home town of Syracuse. In his third year of teaching in an urban middle school, he is loving every second of his new career. And this is obvious to all, when Mr. Salamone describes his new life. "Two wonderful boys and an amazing wife . . . a great family and work that I love. I hit the jackpot!"

Patricia Ruggiano Schmidt is a professor of literacy at Le Moyne College, a Jesuit Institution in Syracuse, New York. After 20 years as a classroom teacher and reading specialist, Schmidt earned her doctorate from the Syracuse University Reading and Language Arts Department. Her research is in the area culturally responsive teaching where she works with elementary and secondary teachers in diverse school settings. Inspired by teacher interests in the improvement of literacy instruction, she designed the model known as the *ABC's of Cultural Understanding and Communication*. Her numerous articles, books, and book chapters often explore the successes of White teachers who develop the self-awareness and appreciation for differences, so necessary for changing the social structures in schools and society. Her studies serve as powerful resources for in-service programs in rural and urban high poverty schools. Dr. Schmidt lives with her husband, Tom, beside a small lake surrounded by the rolling hills of Central New York.

Sharon L. Spencer is the Assistant Dean and Director of Teacher Education in the School of Education at North Carolina Central University. Her B.A. is in Early Childhood Education, M.Ed. in Reading Instruction, and Ph.D. (from the University of North Carolina at Chapel Hill) in Curriculum and Instruction with a focus on Writing. She has been on the faculty since 1990, teaching courses in reading, writing, and mathematics pedagogy. Prior to her tenure at NCCU, she taught for eleven years in the public schools, primarily working at the elementary and middle grades levels in federally funded (Title I) programs. Since 1995, she has been a trainer and instructional support specialist for the National Algebra Project. She is currently principal investigator on a grant to fund the training of teachers in underperforming school districts (from elementary through high school levels) on best practices for teaching writing.

William H. Thelin directs the writing program at the University of Akron and teaches the TA practicum, as well as graduate courses on rhetoric, reading theory, and critical pedagogy. Prior to this, he worked in the open admissions program at the University of Cincinnati, where he participated in a joint effort with the College of Education to give hands-on teaching experience to student candidates in classrooms of at-risk basic writers. His scholarly work can be found in journals such as *College English* and *College Composition and Communication*, and he co-edits the journal *Open Words*, which is dedicated to publishing articles about open admissions and other marginalized populations. He is on the steering committee for the national organization, Rhetoricians for Peace, and is anxiously awaiting the publication of his textbook, *Writing Without Formulas*.

Arlette Ingram Willis received her Ph.D. from the Ohio State University. She is currently a professor at the University of Illinois at Urbana-Champaign in the Department of Curriculum and Instruction, the division of Language and Literacy where she has taught English methods courses for over a decade. Her publications include *Teaching and using multicultural literature in grades 9–12: Moving beyond the canon* (1998) and co-edited books *Multiple and intersecting identities in qualitative research* (with B. Merchant, 2001), *Multicultural issues in literacy research and practice* (with G. Garcia, R. Barrera, and V. Harris), and a forthcoming book *On Critically Conscious Research: Approaches to Language and Literacy Research* (with C. Hunter, M. Montovan, L. Burke, L., A. Herrera, A. and H. Hall, H.) and numerous articles and book chapters.

Sandra A. Vavra received her Ph.D. in Curriculum and Instruction, English Education, from the University of North Carolina at Chapel Hill in 1995. She currently is an Associate Professor of English at North Carolina Central University, where she teaches a variety of writing and methods courses. Sandy is Director of the English Education Program at NCCU, and formerly directed its Writing Center and Composition Program. Her research interests involve teacher preparation, pragmatism and composition, and literacy development. Recent publications include "Put That Red Pen Down, for Now," a chapter in the edited collection *Teacher Commentary* and "Autobiography in Teacher Preparation: The Internally Persuasive Discourse that Speaks with Authority" in the forthcoming book *Building and Imaging Writer: Strategies and Techniques*. She is currently writing a book on brain-friendly teaching strategies with Dr. Sharon Spencer.

Victor Villanueva is the Edward R. Meyer Distinguished Professor of Liberal Arts at Washington State University. His research concerns the interconnectedness among rhetoric (in its broadest sense), ideology, and racism, and their manifestation in literacy and literacy practices. He has written numerous articles and is the editor of *Cross-Talk in Comp Theory*. His book *Bootstraps: From an American Academic of Color* received the National Council of Teachers of English's Russell Award for distinguished research and scholarship in English and the Conference on English Education's Meade Award for scholarship in English Education.

Printed in the United States
90986LV00001B/22-45/A

9 781593 117818